**The Hidden Mysteries for
End Time Hearers Are...**

TOP
SECRET

DR. JACQUELINE LAWRENCE

**The revealing of the Master's
URGENT assignment for His
servants in these last days.**

Copyright © 2006, 2015, 2018, 2019 by Dr. Jacqueline Lawrence.

Library of Congress Control Number: 2006905184

ISBN-13: 978-1-7339594-0-7

All rights reserved. No part of this book may be reproduced or transmitted in any form or by any means, electronic or mechanical, including photocopying, recording, or by any information storage and retrieval system, without permission in writing from the copyright owner.

Scripture quotations marked KJV are from thee Holy Bible, King James Version (Authorized Version). First published in 1611. Quoted from the KJV Classic Reference Bible, Copyright © 1983 by The Zondervan Corporation.

Scripture quotations marked NIV are taken from the Holy Bible, New International Version®. Copyright © 1973, 1978, 1984 by International Bible Society. Used by permission of Zondervan. All rights reserved. [Biblica]

Rev. date:

Published by: J. D. Lawrence Publishing

To share this top-secret message with other believers, order additional copies of this book at: Amazon.com

Let a man so account of us, as of the ministers of Christ, and stewards of the mysteries of God. Moreover it is required in stewards, that a man be found faithful.

1 Corinthians 4:1-2

Matthew 24:15-16 and Mark 13:14 basically say the same thing and are the only two times in the bible where its message is such a profound mystery that God stated, "let the reader understand". Although many prophets and righteous men have longed to see the dreams and visions that Dr. Lawrence has seen, but did not see, and to hear the things that she has heard from God, but did not hear, the Sovereign Lord, who does nothing without revealing His secret to His servants, the prophets, chose to show things that were once hidden from people of previous generations to Jacqueline because NOW is the time for their fulfillment, as these are the last days, and not the days of long ago (Amos 3:7, Isaiah 48: 6b-8).

Dr. Jacqueline Lawrence urges Christians to fulfill our God-ordained. Top Secret assignment in these last days, as was done in the days of Noah

> *All this, said David (Jacqueline), the Lord made me understand in writing by His hand upon me, even all the works of this pattern*
>
> 1 Chronicles 28:19

Because it would be absolutely meaningless for God to give us revelation, knowledge, or prophecy without instructions for carrying out that which He has given us (1 Corinthians 14:6), just as God revealed a specific pattern to Noah for building the Ark, He made known to Dr. Jacqueline Lawrence the pattern of a profound, prophetic, parabolic, and TOP SECRET assignment and network for His saints to unite to build up an end time ark of safety. Christian counselor, author, end time adviser, and most importantly, wise and faithful servant of God, Lawrence obediently feeds God's sheep the very vital message that He gave her. Prophesied as "*The Voice of the Harvest*" (which is the end of the age), Lawrence's mission, like that of Moses and Harriet Tubman, is to help free end time slaves. She strongly urges her Christian brothers and sisters to arise out of their states of complacency and apathy and unite to build up the highway (The way of holiness) for the survival of His great tribulation saints.

And an highway shall be there, and a way, and it shall be called The way of holiness; the unclean shall not pass over it; but it shall be for those: the wayfaring men, though fools, shall not err therein

Isaiah 35:8.

KEEP OUT OF SIGHT, REACH, AND THE HANDS OF SATAN, AS TRULY, THIS BOOK IS...

TOP SECRET

SPECIAL THANKS

I thank the Lord, my everlasting Father and Author and Finisher of my faith, who has made my joy complete by imparting to me the revelation, vision, desire, wisdom, knowledge, love, faithfulness, and understanding necessary to write this prophetic book. My prayer is that the love of those of us to whom the Lord has given ears to hear its vital and urgent message will cause us to obediently and expediently build up the highway, so that servants of God will survive the impending tribulations and great tribulations and stand firm- not only surviving, but thriving- when Jesus returns for us in the clouds.

Having made known unto us the mystery of His will, according to His good pleasure which He hath purposed in Himself: That in the dispensation of the fullness of times He might gather together in one all things in Christ, both which are in heaven, and which are on earth; even in Him.

Ephesians 1:9-10.

CONTENTS

Special Thanks	6
Introduction	8
1. As in the Days of Noah, Sodom, Gomorrah, Katrina...	15
2. Hear Ye! Hear Ye!	37
3. Keep Watch, Be Ready	45
4. End Time Solutions	57
5. Steal Away	85
6. Who Then?	95
7. Preparing for Take-Off	105
References	130
Message From The Author	131

INTRODUCTION

Although many of us might agree that we are approaching the end times, most of us are complacent and unconcerned, and are doing nothing about it. However, more and more, people are beginning to prepare for impending catastrophes. In fact, the term, "prepping" is exploding worldwide, as millions are planning for natural disasters, terrorism, war, disease, and famine. The Spirit of God is infiltrating our nation with information about these end times more now than ever before; just turn on your television, radio, and internet. Unfortunately, much of the information we hear about bible prophecy focuses on highly debatable, fear-induced, and problematic topics over which we have no control, and for which there are no solutions, as opposed to on the need to make preparations for the things to come. However, just as Jesus, because of His love for us, has gone to prepare a place for us, we, too, must love God's children (our brothers and sisters) enough to make preparations for those who will be left behind to endure times of great tribulation.

> *Who then is the faithful and wise servant, whom the master has put in charge of the servants in his household to give them their food at the proper time?*
> Matthew 24:45

Significant circumstances, events, and individuals associated with the end times, such as the tribulation and great tribulation periods, Armageddon, the rapture, the great earthquake, the anti-Christ, beast, and false prophet, are all coming- cut and dry- and there is no amount of prayer that can stop them. The time has come for Christians to stop arguing about times and dates (when the end will take place, when the anti-Christ will arise on the scene, whether the rapture will take place before, during, or after the seven-year tribulation period, whether or not the first resurrection has already occurred), whether or not the beast, false prophet and anti-Christ are the same person, and other discussions that only lead to division, confusion, and distraction. Instead, we must set aside all such topics, and simply do what Jesus told us to do; remain watchful of the signs of the end of the age and of His coming, prayerful about the things that are to come, and ready, so that His sheep can be fed and taken care of during times of great tribulation, and standing firm when He returns.

First comes that which is natural (physical), and then, the things of the spirit (1 Corinthians 15:46), as children of God, we are aware of our Father's natural requirement to feed the hungry, give drink to the thirsty, entertain the stranger, clothe the naked, care for the sick, and visit the imprisoned. We also know that God's very vital spiritual requirement is for us to spread the gospel throughout the nation, so people can hear the messages that the kingdom of God is near, repentance and forgiveness of sins is necessary to attain it, and salvation comes only through Jesus Christ. As we approach the end, however, most people know very little about God's specific requirements for feeding His end time sheep both their natural and spiritual food to fulfill the specific and unique circumstances of the imminent distress, which will be unequal to any other period in history. God's will being done, He intentionally waited for that information to be revealed through this book, by this author, Dr. Jacqueline Lawrence, to you, the reader, and for such a time as this.

> *Whoever obeys His command will come to no harm, and the wise heart will know the proper time and procedure. For there is a proper time and procedure for every matter, though a person may be weighed down by misery.*
>
> - Ecclesiastes 8:5-6 (NIV).

If God had a physical requirement with a proper time and procedure for Noah to build the Ark, Lot and his family to flee from Sodom without looking back, Joseph to store up food in advance of the seven year famine, Moses to raise his staff to set the captives free through a highway called the Red Sea, and Harriet Tubman and other abolitionists to help establish and operate the Underground Railroad by feeding, caring for, and directing runaway slaves through a network of "safe houses" leading north to freedom, you can best believe He has a specific physical requirement with a proper time and procedure for believers in these last days to build an ark of safety so that great tribulation saints will be able to escape the catastrophes of the great tribulation period and stand before the Son of man (Luke 21:36).

If those who do not believe the warnings of Jesus, are uniting to aggressively prepare for the impending disasters- mass deceit, wars, earthquakes, famine, diseases in various places, fearful events and great signs from heaven (Matthew 24:4-8, Luke 21:10) - then surely those of us who say we believe Jesus and His warnings, should be uniting to prepare all the more. And if those who are in the household of faith are preparing for the disasters that are only the beginning of birth pains (deception, wars and rumors of war, national and kingdom divisions, earthquakes, famine, and pestilences, and fearful events and great signs from heaven) how much more should we be making preparations for the second and third trimester birth pains (that period of time which Jesus warned us will be more devastating than any other period in history, and finally the arrival of our Lord and Savior, Jesus Christ in the clouds (Matthew 24:15-31)?

Oftentimes, preachers teach that during what is commonly known as the great tribulation period, one must be willing to give up his life for Christ. It is true. Certainly, one must, should it become necessary. And for some, it will be (Daniel 11:33). However, because God gave Noah, Joseph, Lot, Moses, and Harriet a plan to escape the catastrophes in their day, and because Jesus made a way for us to live abundantly (John 10:10), and because going into captivity in that day may be an option (Revelation 13:10), and because we are expected to stand when we see Jesus return for us in the clouds, then we must understand that our God not only has a plan of escape for us, but He also has a plan for us to live an abundant life, to be free from captivity, and to survive great tribulations even unto the end.

CHAPTER 1

AS IN THE DAYS OF NOAH, SODOM, GOMORRAH, KATRINA...

For the Son of Man in His day will be like the lightning, which flashes and lights up the sky from one end to the other.

But first He must suffer many things and be rejected by this generation.

Just as it was in the days of Noah, so also will it be in the days of the Son of Man.

People were eating, drinking, marrying and being given in marriage up to the day Noah entered the Ark. Then the flood came and destroyed them all.

It was the same in the days of Lot. People were eating and drinking, buying and selling, planting and building.

But the day Lot left Sodom, fire and sulfur rained down from heaven and destroyed them all.

Luke 17:24-29 (NIV).

For if God did not spare angels when they sinned, but sent them to hell, putting them in chains of darkness to be held for judgment;

if He did not spare the ancient world when He brought the flood on its ungodly people, but protected Noah, a preacher of righteousness, and seven others;

if He condemned the cities of Sodom and Gomorrah by burning them to ashes, and made them an example of what is going to happen to the ungodly;

and if He rescued Lot, a righteous man, who was distressed by the depraved conduct of the lawless

(for that righteous man, living among them day after day, was tormented in his righteous soul by the lawless deeds he saw and heard)—

if this is so, then the Lord knows how to rescue the godly from trials and to hold the unrighteous for punishment on the day of judgment

2 Peter 2:4-9.

After forming each of His creations, from the first through the fifth day- the light, heavens, earth and seas, the grass, herbs and fruit trees, the sun, moon and stars, water creatures and winged fowl, the beasts, cattle and every creeping thing- God was so pleased that He, Himself proclaimed that they were all "good". It was not until after He completed His final creation- when He made man and woman on the sixth day- that He saw that everything He created was "**very** good". In fact, He thought so highly of His creation of man and woman that He told us to have dominion over all the animals and to be fruitful and multiply so that we would subdue the whole earth and become more numerous than the sand of the sea and the stars in the sky. How He must have loved us! How pleased He must have been with His work! What awesome plans He must have had for us!

When man began to increase in number, every inclination of his heart being evil from childhood, they began marrying anyone they chose. In the days of Noah, because of man's sinful ways, the Lord became grieved and pained by the fact that He even created man. Refusing to leave the guilty unpunished, God decided to wipe out every living thing, with the exception of Noah, who was a righteous man, his family, and seven pairs of every kind of clean animals and every kind of bird, and one pair of every kind of unclean animal (Genesis 7:2-3). He instructed Noah to build an Ark so that he and his family could evacuate the devastating flood that He was about to pour on the land. In holy fear, Noah condemned the world and became heir of the righteousness that comes by faith, and when warned about things not yet seen, he built an Ark to avoid the flood waters and the storm according to the pattern given to Him by God so that he could save his family, the animals, and the birds.

The devastating 2004 Indian Ocean earthquake commonly known as "The Tsunami", provides us with somewhat of a visual of the many dead bodies that must have been floating amidst the flood waters. What a dreadful sight to see and disgusting odor to behold! Similarly, how silenced the whole earth must have been once the storm subsided; no cattle roaming, no creeping things creeping, no birds chirping, and no people marrying and giving in marriage, eating and drinking, and taking life easy. Because, with the exception of those in the Ark, everything that moved on the earth had perished, and due to the fact that vultures gather where dead bodies exist (Luke 17:37), one can only imagine the feast the vultures must have had when released from the Ark.

After the flood, God promised never again to curse the ground and destroy all living things by flood waters, but that next time, He would execute judgment upon those who do not walk in His ways with plague and bloodshed. He said that He would pour down on them torrents of rain, turning the rain into hailstones with lightening and burning sulfur, like He did in the days of Sodom and Gomorrah when every young and old man from Sodom tried engaging in homosexual relations with Lot's two male visitors (Genesis 19:4-5). Because the outcry against people in most cities today is grievously sinful, just as they were in the days of Noah, Sodom, and Gomorrah, many believe that the time for God to execute His judgment is once again, upon us. Destructive forces which lead to idol worshipping in the form of lies, drugs and alcohol, gambling, theft, violence, prostitution, unjust gain, sexual immorality, greed, violence, injustice, corruption, selfishness, hatred, pride, prejudice, racism, and all kinds of wickedness, can be easily seen at work all over the world in cities that were once faithful, just, and righteous, but have now become harlots, murderous, built with bloodshed, and established by crime.

The city of New Orleans, for example, well known throughout the world for its rich Cajun and Creole cuisine, Bourbon Street, Mardi Gras, bayous, beads, French Quarters, and all that jazz, attracts those who parade their sins of sexual immorality, lawlessness, perversion, adultery, lies, wickedness, arrogance, greed, witchcraft, unconcern, and selfishness. As in the days of Noah, when men were having sex with anyone they chose- married and unmarried, same and opposite sex, child and adult, animal and human, dead and alive, with and without consent, spouse and stranger, family member and non-family member- serving as a model of those who will suffer the punishment of eternal fire because of their great wickedness, God sent Katrina. This massive Hurricane came hurling in on August 29, 2005, taking thousands of lives in Louisiana, Mississippi and Alabama. Hardest hit, however, was the city of New Orleans, disintegrating the popular homosexual festival, Southern Decadence, also known as the "Gay Mardi Gras", which is held annually during the Labor Day weekend. Perhaps symbolizing God's fierce anger toward Himself and regret for ever commanding Noah to build the Ark so that the lives of this sinful generation could be spared, when unscrambled, Katrina might support the notion of an "Anti-Ark".

Some believe that as a punishment to the city of New Orleans, God loaded the clouds with moisture, causing them to turn around and around under His direction, and flashed them with His lightening. Because of its sinfulness, God caused the city to become a mockery- an object of scorn- by pulling its skirt over its face and tearing it off so that its adulterous shame, lustful neighings, and prostitution could be seen as a modern day reminder of the devastation that has been prophesied to penetrate the entire earth. Surely those from near and far were shocked at how the infamous, carefree city was turned into such turmoil, left in ruins, battered to pieces, and because so many forgot the Lord and trusted in false gods, was scattered like chaff driven by the desert wind; its elders gone from the city gate, the music of its young men, stopped.

So angry with the people of New Orleans and cities like it because of their detestable acts, if God chose to do so, He could have destroyed the entire world with Katrina, Tina, Regina, or anyone He pleased. But being one with His word, He promised that never again would He destroy the world by flood. Instead, being kept for the Day of Judgment and destruction of ungodly men, He has reserved the present heavens and earth for fire a fire, which some believe, has already been kindled (2 Peter 3:7 NIV). Still, many do not recognize the time of His coming, that day when every stone of His Holy Temple and all the children within their walls, will be dashed to the ground. Although the stage is perfectly set for such a day, it is only because of God's grace that He has been holding out in hopes that we would hurry up and be ready. Time, however, is running out, and although no man knows the day or hour, we do know that He will not wait forever.

In spite of much warning and advice about what was, is, and is to come, many people have eyes that only see what they want to see, and ears that hear only what they want to hear. Although God wants us to see and hear with spiritual, as opposed to only natural eyes and ears, so that we will be able to discern and understand the things of His Spirit, many, being stubborn, do not allow God to open their hearts so that they can see and hear through His eyes and ears. Sometimes, when warnings and advice are given about those things that are likely to harm or hinder people, only a few really even want to get an understanding of them. Many get offended and become defensive when good, sound advice is given. The harvest being plentiful, but laborers, few, some fail to allow warnings and advice to penetrate their hearts, fearing that they would clearly see and hear, and would be expected to not only become hearers, but more importantly, doers.

There have been more than enough occasions when all of us, at one time or another, have been stubborn and refused to take heed to God's warnings and advice. When He has shown and told us things for our own good- to help us, and not to harm us- there have been times when each of us did not want to hear or see what He had to reveal to us because we stubbornly only wanted to see with our own eyes and hear with our own ears, leaning to our own understanding, so that we could continue directing our own paths. God has given us more than enough warning and advice. His holy word being saturated with profound, parabolic, and prophetic mysteries, understanding them, requires faith. Because faith without works is dead, we must work out the things we believe, with our hands, as believing without doing, is self-deceptive and meaningless.

One of the things about which God has warned us is the many devastating hurricanes that are destined to come upon the earth in these last days (Luke 21:25). Hurricane Katrina, for example, is one such hurricane. Denoting "purification", God employed her to warn us to purify, or clean up, our act. Upon her approach, inasmuch as people were warned and advised to evacuate from their hometowns, many, believing that they would not be affected by her, chose not to evacuate. Thousands who remained in the city of New Orleans, failed to follow instructions for one reason or another. They were then commanded to flee to the Louisiana Superdome, a large sports stadium located in downtown New Orleans. Still, many failed to obey.

Because those who made the decision to congregate inside the Superdome were surrounded by flood waters and stranded there for several days, they were without adequate food, water, air conditioning, flushing toilets, toilet paper, water, lights, cots, bedding, security, identification, linen, medical assistance, and other basic necessities. What a horrific sight to see and horrendous odor to smell! An evacuation plan, we learned, must consist of more than just a place to re-house people, but must provide a safe shelter away from the anticipated devastation. In the event of an anticipated flood, this shelter may need to be located on higher terrain, as opposed to on level ground, so that help may be able to arrive in a timely manner.

These individuals, who were primarily African American, did not take heed to warnings and advice to evacuate from their city, and adequate provisions were not made for them at the proper time, which would have been prior to the evacuation. Therefore, many suffered, and there was much weeping and gnashing of teeth. Who could have imagined that something so dreadful would have occurred in the great city of New Orleans, in this great nation, and in this great generation of modern science, information, technology, and "intelligence"? In hindsight, had the victims of Katrina known about all the destruction and peril that would lie ahead for them, they most likely would have prepared themselves for the looming devastation by taking heed to warnings and advice to evacuate. Had they known their homes would have been wiped out, perhaps they would have taken more of their personal belongings with them on their journey. Had it been the last time they would have seen their loved ones, maybe- just maybe- they would have shown them more love when they had the opportunity. Had they known there would have been inadequate provisions prepared for them at the Superdome, they, themselves, almost certainly would have taken more food, water, blankets, pillows, flashlights, batteries, generators, medical, and other supplies. Had they established an emergency evacuation plan in advance in the event that some loved ones might become lost or separated from their families, perhaps some would not have gone missing for so long.

We must anticipate that future catastrophes will result in numerous deaths and unidentifiable bodies. As in the case of Hurricane Katrina, for example, where New Orleans evacuees were prevented from returning to their city immediately after the hurricane due to unsafe conditions (no available power, potable water, operating stores, hospitals, or gas stations), many of the deceased who refused to evacuate neither out of the city nor to the Superdome, could not be identified for a long period of time. Some of the bodies that were discovered quite some time after the levees broke were so decomposed that they, being beyond recognition, were unidentifiable. Many sex offenders and parolees who were forced to take flight could not be tracked, and thus, could not be found. Many of our young, aged, and disabled who were relocated to various shelters or were otherwise missing, were separated from their families and caretakers, and were unable to identify themselves, not to mention, their caretakers.

Because of the fact that future devastations will cause many to lose their lives, and because of the rise of identity theft, it has been predicted that government officials will soon begin to enforce the utilization of a marking system, which will likely be linked to social security numbers, DNA, or a similar form of identification. In fact, because of the lack of such a system, and because of the devastating events that occurred with Katrina, officials were so convinced that death would be inevitable for many who refused to evacuate from Hurricane Rita, the hurricane that occurred in the Houston area only one month after Katrina hit, that they urged Houstonians to place their identification cards inside one of their socks or write their social security numbers on one of their arms, so that when their bodies were discovered, they could be easily identified. With the advancement of modern technology, surely officials are making more forward-thinking plans than this.

Many believe this marking system could possibly be a biochip placed in the palm of the hand or on the forehead similar to that used to identify, track, and/or brand animals, garments, automobiles, and the like. Others believe an iris scanning devise, or other form of identification mechanism, will be used over the forehead. It is also believed that such a mark will identify individuals at banks, ATM machines, stores, airports, and anywhere that people go to buy or sell things. Most Christians believe this mark is deceitful, its root stemming from greed, pride, prejudice, and power, and has nothing at all to do with helping, but hurting mankind. This impending worldly system may symbolize the scripture, John 6:66, which depicts the turning back and away of many of Christ's disciples from Him, and is likely a precursor to the mark of the beast, which is 666 (Revelation 13:18).

Due to the fact that Katrina, in and of itself, was not as devastating as some had anticipated she would be, many of those who chose not to evacuate from their homes, were most likely relieved that they were not inconvenienced by either of the mandatory flights to "safety". Then, no sooner had they set their feet on the ground, did the levees break loose and the waters of Lake Ponchartrain come rushing in much worse than the flood. Because it was only after the waters receded that help became available, many, unfortunately, lost their lives.

God's power being displayed in the whirlwind and the storm (Nahum 1:3), our reaction to His power is also displayed in the whirlwind and the storm. Although some Katrina victims had no way of evacuating, neither from their city nor to the Superdome, due to a lack of finances, transportation, assistance, and the like, still others took the pending devastation as a joke, just as Lot's sons-in-law did when they were told to hurry and evacuate from Sodom and Gomorrah because the Lord was about to destroy their city (Genesis 19:12-14). Many, therefore, perished because of their lack of knowledge. They did not know their ignorance and the wickedness that went in and came out of their mouths as a result of their ignorance, would cause them to perish. They did not know that waiting until the last minute to evacuate would not allow them enough time to get out. Like Lot's wife, some did not know that if they looked back at what had always been home, refusing to flee from the sinful desires of the heart of their city, that their bodies would become stubbornly frozen in the waters, like pillars of salt.

Through Katrina, God revealed that inasmuch as some people live their lives as though they do not care whether they live or die, ignoring everything they have heard about keeping the way of the Lord and doing what is just and right, when faced with death, they often do all they can to hold on to their lives, and to God. Some of those in New Orleans, for example, as in the days of Noah, Sodom and Gomorrah, had been living their lives as though they had never heard of God. But when the levees broke and the thought of losing their lives entered their minds, the first thing that flew out of their mouths was, "Oh, my God! Save me!" When trapped inside the Superdome and on rooftops for days without food, water, showers, and toilets, in their anger, many likely turned away from Him, screaming, and "God damn it!" Later, when rescuers finally came to save them, I wonder how many lifted up their face toward heaven to say, "Thank God!" Even though some may live their lives as though they could care less about whether they live or die, most, I believe, desire to live as long as possible. All too often, however, many are more concerned about living long, mortal lives that have an imminent expiration date, than about living eternal lives. Many are afraid of death and do not even discuss the subject, as though avoiding it will cause them to escape it.

Less than a month after we witnessed the devastating effects of Katrina, before our grief had turned to joy, the Lord, who turns blackness into dawn and darkens day into night, who calls for the waters of the sea and pours them out over the face of the land, who flashes destruction on the stronghold and brings the fortified city to ruin, dispatched a major threat to the city of Houston by the name of "Hurricane Rita". Upon Rita's approach, and in spite of what they had just witnessed with Katrina, some, following the stubbornness of their hearts, chose to "ride out the storm"; as if it were some wild animal that could be tamed, as if we could say to the wind, storm, and rain, "Stop!", and they will obey. How dare we have the audacity to think we have the power to prosper in any storm without God's grace, and without proper preparation!

Rita, her name meaning "pearl", which is a gem recognized as the emblem of purity, confirmed God's warning for us to purify ourselves- become humble, pray, seek His face, and turn from our wicked ways, so He could hear from heaven, forgive our sin, and heal our land. Thankfully, in her last hours, just before advancing toward land, she slowed her roll, sympathetically decreasing in intensity, and turned away from Houston to shed light on God's mercy toward us, and His unfailing love for us.

Another issue on which both Katrina and Rita shed light, is the fact that because of predictable business shut downs that are bound to arise during mandatory evacuations, no one will be able to buy or sell anything from businesses in cities that have been evacuated. Therefore, during major catastrophes, in addition to an increase in looting and violence, one can always expect the unavailability of emergency services and vital necessities such as food, water, gasoline, and emergency supplies. The establishment of a plan to ascertain the availability of these necessities for potentially millions, in the event of a mandatory evacuation, therefore, is vital. Additionally, as could be clearly seen in the case of Hurricane Rita, where millions of people were trapped on over-congested freeways in their plight to take flight from Houston, an evacuation plan must afford evacuees (including those in hospitals, prisons, and other institutions) the opportunity to leave their cities safely and within a reasonable timeframe, and to have access to emergency services.

Even though both Hurricane Rita and Katrina shed light on America's ignorance, the problems associated with our emergency evacuation system, ill-preparedness, and vulnerability to extreme disaster, they also shed light on our ability to achieve that which needs to be accomplished when we are all on one accord. I was blessed to have had the opportunity to provide prayer and financial support to some of the Katrina evacuees who were transported to the Convention Center in Dallas, Texas. The fond memories of the amazing outpouring of support of loving, generous, and caring individuals, churches, ministries, businesses, and organizations that helped those whose lives had been turned upside down, will forever remain in my heart. Outside the center were long lines of cars of people who were eager to donate new items of clothing, shoes, hygiene and grooming supplies, linen, blankets, pillows, books, toys, medical and emergency equipment, food, water, diapers, and the like.

There was such a long line of volunteers standing outside the Convention Center, who were waiting for the opportunity to get inside to provide help and comfort, that a waiting list was developed, so that when one exited the building, another could enter. From outside, one could hear the voice of a man inside the building who was speaking on a microphone. Similar to that of an aggressive auctioneer, he was yelling out the addresses and descriptions of various apartments that had been donated to the evacuees. Once God graciously allowed me permission to enter the building- without having to get on the waiting list due to the favor that He placed upon me for this mission- I expected to see a mob of forceful people shoving their way toward the auctioneer to obtain the free apartments. Instead, the auctioneer stood all alone, in a corner, the housing needs of the evacuees, obviously met. In addition to housing opportunities, a variety of jobs, intercessory prayer, counseling, and other free services were plentiful to meet the needs of the evacuees. Most walked around listlessly, shaking their heads, "No" in response to the repeated offerings of bottled water, popsicles, and other items of comfort from the blistering heat. Some humbly gathered clothing and other needed items from the large piles on the floor. All, although extremely devastated, seemed grateful to be alive.

Not one ignored my offering for prayer. I was very pleased to see how grateful they were for the support of people throughout the Dallas/Fort Worth Metroplex who gave of their money, donations, and time. Even though some were devastated about the loss of deceased and missing loved ones, most, like the "Whos" of "Whoville" whose Christmas presents were taken away by the Grinch in the popular Christmas cartoon, <u>How The Grinch Stole Christmas</u>, seemed hopeful that all that had happened to their great city, their homes, their families, and their lives, would somehow work together for their good. Many, with apparent sincerity of heart, dedicated and/or re-dedicated their lives to Christ.

People all over the world heard the warnings and advice for New Orleans residents to evacuate, as well as the news about the thousands who lost their lives for refusing to comply with instructions to take flight. After Katrina hit, many throughout the world, began preparing themselves, both spiritually and naturally, for the inevitable catastrophes to come- renewing their faith in God, storing up necessities, and developing evacuation plans. Because of the stubborn hearts of some of the New Orleanians, prayerfully, we have all learned to take heed to warnings of disaster and advice to evacuate much more seriously and to remain watchful of, and ready for impending disasters. May this lack of planning be a lesson for all of us to keep watch of, and be ready for, not only the exponential increase and intensification of catastrophes caused by "Mother Nature", as some call "Him", but also, the famine, plague, persecutions, and bloodshed about which we have been warned for generations (Matthew 24, Mark 13, Luke 21).

Although the beauty of mankind pulling together to feed and take care of God's sheep could be seen around the world, unfortunately, the storm also revealed some darkened hearts. Some local residents in and around Dallas, and most certainly other places of refuge, deceitfully attempting to identify themselves as victims of Katrina in an effort to benefit from the catastrophe, attained free debit cards, apartments, jobs, food, clothing, false identifications, medical care, and other similar benefits. Some of our nation's onlookers, who were racially prejudice against blacks, offered very little, if any, assistance because, resembling a third world country, it was clear that most of the evacuees were African Americans. Immediately turning the television channel from the news about the destruction, as though it were a meaningless commercial, many who were not personally affected by the storm, continued on with their lives as though the devastation meant nothing to them. Through Katrina, therefore, we have also learned that help may not be as readily available for some, as it is for others. Some groups, therefore, will likely need to unite to develop plans for themselves, as they may not be able to depend on the government or general public for assistance.

Exactly seven years following the destruction of Hurricane Katrina, came yet another dreadful hurricane to the city of New Orleans, again, threatening, but this time, not halting the celebrants of the Gay Mardi Gras, who laughed in its face. Isaac, which means, "He will laugh", embodying the fact that God will have the last laugh, was no joking matter. In Proverbs 1:22-27, God warned those who are mockers, simple, and foolish, that because they refuse to listen when He calls, pay attention when He stretches out His hand, disregard His advice, and accept His rebuke when disaster strikes them, He will also laugh at their calamity, and mock them when terror comes like a storm, destruction sweeps over them like a whirlwind, and when distress and trouble overwhelms them.

Having been warned and advised for centuries to maintain food, water, emergency supplies, and an updated evacuation plan for future catastrophes, Katrina being a crisis of the past, most continue to ignore the warning, and continue existing as though she never did. Through His word, God has not only been warning us to prepare to evacuate from catastrophes that will take place in these end times, but also, to evacuate from the world. He told us to keep ourselves from being polluted by the world (James 1:27) and to separate ourselves from unbelievers (2 Corinthians 6:17). Hearing the warning, and even seeing the warning signs, many do not fear God enough to evacuate from the world and its anxieties, the desires of the flesh, and from unbelievers. Just as the people in the days of Noah did not fear the flood waters enough to build themselves an ark, Lot's sons-in-law laughed and took warnings and advice to evacuate as a joke, and those in New Orleans and Houston refused to evacuate, and even laughed in the face of calamity, many today, even those who call themselves Christians, refuse to prepare for imminent dangers today, let alone, for those that are destined to occur during times of great tribulations.

Although the gospel of Jesus Christ has likely been preached all over the world, signifying the end (Matthew 24:14), and people have been warned that if they continue to live sinful lives, they will not inherit the kingdom of God, still, many close their ears, and do not listen. Taking it as a joke, they find the word of God to be offensive and unpleasant, and thus, they shun God, and not evil. Those who love the world and the ways of the world choose not to evacuate from the world and to holy and higher ground, but to remain in their sinfulness and complacency, and therefore, will end up losing out on eternal life.

The Bible tells us that in these last days, deception, wars, rumors of wars, national and kingdom divisions, famines, earthquakes, and diseases are just the beginning of birth pains (Matthew 24:4-8). Not only do we need to take all necessary precautions for ourselves and for our loved ones, but like the loving, caring, and kind people all over the world who helped Katrina, Rita, Tsunami, Haiti, Isaac, Sandy and other victims during their times of tribulation, we need to prepare children of God all over the world for the great tribulations that lie ahead. Like those who were stubbornly left behind in New Orleans to endure the atrocities of Katrina, and like all of us who have been stubborn at one time or another, many in this adulterous generation do not listen to God's warnings and advice, but are waiting for a sign that will affect them enough to take heed- perhaps another major catastrophe, the death of a loved one, the rapture (the sudden gathering together of saints in the air to meet Jesus), or even the Second Coming of Christ.

God's Word tells us that Jesus is coming soon, and even though most, if not all of us, have heard the message, still, many refuse to evacuate from this world to eternal life through the blood of Jesus Christ.

Therefore, we, who are loving, caring, kind, faithful, wise, pure, and upright, not knowing when God will rouse Himself from His Holy dwelling on our behalf to restore us to our rightful place, must bear the infirmities of the weak, and make preparations for God's servants who are unprepared. Inasmuch as God commands us to listen to Him and follow His ways in order that our peace would be like a river and our righteousness, like the waves of the sea, still, many rebel and grieve His Holy Spirit. They reject Him when He calls and do not give heed when He stretches out His hand, but ignores His advice. It is likely accurate for us to conclude that God continues to be sick and tired of being sick and tired of warning us about the need for us to obey Him, and about the things that will happen to us if we fail to do so. Just as God's grace prevailed over the lives of thousands of Katrina victims who successfully rode out the storm in spite of their stubbornness to evacuate, the world's very existence is riding on God's grace.

We have heard over and over again that the world as we know it will one day end. We have been warned that the kingdom of God is at hand and that if we are not saved, we will go to hell. We have been advised to accept Jesus Christ, the only begotten Son of God, as our Lord and Savior. We have been told to believe in our hearts and confess with our mouths that because of His love for us, Christ died, and was resurrected on the third day with all power in His hand to take away our sins, so that through His grace and by our faith in Him, we can be saved. In spite of these continuous warnings and advice, still, many remain ignorant, and refuse to evacuate to eternal life. Prayerfully, like the righteous Noah, God's children will take heed to His warnings and advice to spiritually evacuate from this world and to obey His implied command to develop evacuation plans for imminent, natural dangers in these last days, such as those in the days of Noah, Sodom, Gomorrah, and Katrina.

AS IN THOSE DAYS

In Noah's day, people were focused
on drinking and eating their food,
taking life easy, having sex with anyone they chose,
being merry, and lewd.

The Lord was so grieved
with sinful man
that He destroyed all but the righteous
according to His plan.

As in those days, many are wicked,
immoral, and deceitful today,
laughing at warnings of calamity
and refusing to obey.

Warn them that He's coming once again
to carry off His house;
righteous men,
their children and their spouses.

Let them know that when devastation comes
to destroy them all,
God is the only one
who can answer their call.

Warn them that after Jesus returns
to claim His own,
through His wrath, He will rain down
fire and brimstone.

Advise everyone
to escape the burning sulfur;
not after, but before
the great devastation occurs.

Prepare yourself and your brother
for that evil day.
Build arks of safety NOW,
before it's too late.

Flee to the mountains
for a place to hide.
Plan to live,
but be willing to die.

CHAPTER 2

HEAR YE! HEAR YE!

Concerning the end times, because biblical prophecies are difficult to timeline and most of what we hear deals with the doom, gloom, despair, mayhem, panicky defeatism, woes, catastrophes, and devastation, over which we have little to no control, people tend to flee from such discussions. When those who are bold enough to delve into eschatological dialogue, take the plunge, such dialogue often leads to arguments and debates about who the anti-Christ will be, how the world will end, and times and dates of the occurrence of significant end time events such as the rapture, Armageddon, the tribulation period, and Jesus' Second Coming. Because studies, sermons, and discussions surrounding the end times are oftentimes lightly approached, and even avoided, inaccurate information, division, confusion, and ultimately, apathy and complacency typically surface. Although the many signs of the end are unfolding right before our very eyes, most do not even think about the end times, let alone, about preparing for them.

This, the 21st century, is known as "the information age", as we are provided with ample opportunities for increased knowledge. The expansion in technology readily avails massive and easily accessible information about the end times. Bibles are oftentimes given away for free. Knowledge about every topic under, around, and above the sun is right at our fingertips, on the internet, television, radio, newspapers, magazines, and books, yet, people still ask basic questions of others because they are too lazy to study for themselves and show themselves approved. We say we want certain information, but frequently, even when the information is given to us, we are either not listening, or we allow it to go right over our heads without doing anything to even try to grab hold of it. Therefore, it is not enough for us to hear the information, we must act out that which we hear, for not doing so, is meaningless.

Given the title as "Watchman" over Israel (Ezekiel 3:17), in the Olivet Discourse (Matthew 24, Mark 13, and Luke 21), Jesus warned the house of Israel about the signs of the end of the age and of His coming, sharing the weightier matters, those events for which, although we cannot control, we can, and are expected, to prepare. Therefore, those things which Jesus, Himself deemed important enough about which to warn us regarding the end times, should also be our primary focus.

After He rode into Jerusalem on a donkey, Jesus spoke to the crowd in parables for the last time, warning them of the hypocrisy and woes of the false teachers and Pharisees, while dodging their alleged traps. He made it known that they would not see Him again until they say, "Blessed is He who comes in the name of the Lord" on that blessed day when every knee will bow and every tongue will confess His Lordship over all mankind (Matthew 23:39, Romans 14:11). Once the crowd paid their offerings and as Jesus was leaving the temple, Peter, James, John and Andrew came to Him privately. The first thing they wanted to know was WHEN the Jewish temple would be destroyed, and WHAT would be the signs that all these things would come to pass (Matthew 24:1-3). I can imagine how their ears must have been open wide with the hope of hearing the full revelation of a precise date and time when these things would take place. But having come to know Jesus as they did, although He explained everything that belonged to them (Mark 4:34, Deuteronomy 29:29), which was more than when He spoke to the crowds, reality most likely told them that He would leave them with something on which to ponder, as was typical for Him to do.

Jesus' disciples understood that when He spoke openly to the crowds, although everyone could hear Him with their natural ears- those who were not deaf, of course- He often used a secret, parabolic, figurative, and implied figure of speech to reveal secrets hidden since the creation of the world, so that not everyone would understand, but only those to whom He had given ears; His sheep. When He spoke privately with His disciples, however, He trusted them with the mysteries revealed by God, and even though He would typically leave them with something to challenge their thinking, they knew to accept His answer as being completely and intentionally revealed because the knowledge of the secrets of the kingdom of heaven was given to them, but not to unbelievers.

On several occasions, when speaking to the crowd, Jesus said, "Who hath ears to hear, let him hear" (Matthew 13:43). He said this because the creator of ears, eyes, and minds did not give everyone ears to hear, eyes to see, and a mind to understand. The ears of those who do not belong to God are not open to hear His words, which must be spiritually discerned, because to them, His word is foolish and offensive, and they find no pleasure in it. A breed of senseless fools, they exist in a spirit of stupor, and because they are unable to grasp the things of God, and are even afraid to ask about them so they can get an understanding of them, they remain in a stupor. Turning their ears from the truth and toward myths to suit their own desires, they hear only what they want to hear (2 Timothy 3:4).

Those who are God's sheep not only hear His secret things, but they hide them in their hearts so they do not sin against Him, obeying that which they hear. Because His servants can be relied upon to follow Him, He entrusts them with His hidden mysteries that He destined for our glory before time began (1 Corinthians 2:4-7). He does not speak His words solely for the benefit of the hearer, but so that His reliable servants will teach others, speaking in the daylight, what He tells them in the dark, and proclaiming from the rooftops, what is whispered in their ear (Matthew 10:27).

It is not enough for us to merely hear, but believe and stand firm in that which our ears spiritually discern, being strong and uncompromising when we are being tested, and refraining from worrying about worldly things, lest the devil come along and snatch what we have heard, and we no longer believe. Once God's words are heard and even received with joy, if they are not put into practice, hearing becomes ineffective, and that which has been heard can easily be snatched away. We must therefore, not only be hearers, but exercise that which we hear by becoming doers of it. Hearing without doing is like building a house with no foundation; for a house without a foundation will collapse and be destroyed the minute a storm hits (Luke 6:49).

CAN YOU HEAR HIM?

I hope that you can hear Him.
I hope that you're His sheep.
That land of milk and honey,
I pray you'll someday reap.

I hope that you can hear Him,
I'm checking out your fruit.
I'm thinking that He knows you,
but sometimes, I get fooled.

Do you know His secrets;
His deep and hidden things?
When He speaks His words unto you,
Does it make your spirit sing?

It's not enough to hear His words,
you must be a doer, too,
for merely hearing, without doing,
is not maturing you.

Do you belong to the Father?
Is He the Ruler of your life?
Even in your darkest hour,
can you still see His light?

If you can't hear when He speaks to you,
Ask Him to clean your ears
so you may know His mysteries
and walk in faith, not fear.

CHAPTER 3
KEEP WATCH, BE READY

Jesus lived on this earth for thirty-three years- healing, delivering, dying, and after three days, rising to prepare a place for us- so that by His grace and through our faith, those of us who were once captivated by sin, could be set free to live with Him, throughout eternity. Just as He has made it a priority to prepare a beautiful home in His kingdom for us, we must be about our Father's end time business and prepare for Him when He returns to take us to that home in glory, by keeping the household of faith watchful and ready for His return.

Today, people speak so complacently about Jesus' Second Coming, as though it is business as usual. Some Christians do not even warn others about this most phenomenal event in the history of all mankind, but casually make remarks about it as though a distant relative is visiting for a family reunion. Many treat the event of Jesus' return to take us to paradise to be with Him forever as though it is no big deal. Huge issues are made about, and a major amount of finances and preparation is devoted to prominent, worldly events such as the NFL Super Bowl, Presidential Elections, Academy Awards, Boston Marathon, Kentucky Derby, Macy's Thanksgiving Day Parade, and even for special occasions in our personal lives, such as vacations, weddings, funerals, and family reunions. But the event of Jesus' Second Coming has succumbed to a very selfish way of thinking. People typically either reason, "I am saved, therefore, I am not worried about it because I'll either be dead or raptured up, anyways", "I am not sure if I am saved, and would rather not think about it", or "I could care less, because if He's coming, He isn't coming for me".

Not only do we not spend time meditating on, visualizing, fantasizing, and glorifying in this most significant, impending event like we do other meaningful events in our lives, most do not even think about preparing for Jesus' return. If we make natural preparations for other momentous occasions in our lives, then as believers who are looking forward to the Second Coming of Christ, surely we, as one body, should make plans and preparations for the arrival of our Lord and Savior, Jesus Christ.

We are devoted to uniting to make decisions about when and where our family reunions will be held, for example, what activities will take place, who will be in charge of the food, program, music, and games, and who will accommodate specified out-of-town guests, for whom we go through great lengths to impress. Remaining watchful of, and ready for the arrival of our visitors, we do all we can to make sure our homes are immaculate, fragrant, and neat; fresh bed linen smoothed on the beds, clean towels hung in the restrooms, refrigerators and essentials well-stocked, delicious meals prepared and hot, vacuum line designs displayed on carpets, the aroma of air freshener, incense, and candles filling our rooms, family members and inside pets well-groomed, cars washed and gassed up, and children well-informed of our behavioral expectations of them. If we can come together to go out of our way to prepare for and please our out-of-town family members, how much more should we unite to prepare for our family reunion on the day that we see our Big Brother coming for us in the clouds?

In order for us to prepare for Jesus' Second Coming, we must first arise from complacency, denial, and apathy by seeing this affair as one that is just as real as, and even more significant than any other major, future incident that we believe will take place and to which we are looking forward with great anticipation. Secondly, we must unite to make plans as one people speaking the same language so that our plans will prosper (Genesis 11:6). And thirdly, we must faithfully be doers of all that we hear (James 1:22).

When asked if they are ready for the end times, most Christians, thinking that they are being asked if they are spiritually "ready", believe what they are being asked is, "Are you saved?" Without giving much thought to the question, they affirm that they are, in fact, "ready". Being saved, however, means declaring with one's mouth that Jesus is Lord, and believing in one's heart that God raised Him from the dead (Romans 10:9). Even though some may believe that being ready for the end times is synonymous with being saved, some of these so-called "ready" individuals do not love others enough to give one thought about spreading the good news of Jesus Christ. In fact, some of these individuals who claim to be ready for the end times, simply because they have provided lip service, calling Jesus, "Lord, Lord" with their mouths, have not committed themselves to believing in their hearts that Jesus is Lord over their lives, as evidenced by refusing to turn from sin and follow Him. Unless these individuals repent and turn to God with their whole heart, not only will they not be saved, they will also not be ready to enter the kingdom of God, but will be cut to pieces (Matthew 24:48-51).

I'M CUTTING YOU TO PIECES

You had your chance.
I brought My gospel to you.
But you maintained your wicked ways,
and would not hear Me.
Even though I loved you,
and gave up My life for you,
you rejected Me.
You didn't love the Father
or the brother.
I have to cast you down and out.

You had your chance.
You would not accept Me.
You turned your back away from Me
and stopped up your ears,
so you could not hear Me.
You would not fear Me.
You heard the trumpet sound,
but you did not take warning,
so I will judge your evil practices,
and let your blood be on your own head.

The ax is already at the root of the trees,
and every tree that does not produce good fruit
will be cut down and thrown into the fire.
Not a root or a branch will be left to you.
I will rain down bloodshed and fiery coals;
a scorching wind will be your lot.
On that day, it will be so very hot.
There will be torrents of rain, hailstones and burning sulfur.
I'll place you with the wicked.
There will be weeping and gnashing of teeth.

The end has come rousing itself against you.
You will be thrown outside in the darkness.
There will be panic; doom will come upon you.
I will strike you with the sword, with famine, diseases
and all kinds of plagues until you perish.
You, like the trash on the ground, will not be mourned or buried.
Your body will be food for the vultures and the beasts of the earth.
Then I will say, "Depart from Me, into the eternal fire
that I have prepared for the devil and his angels."
And I will put all My enemies under My feet.

I'm cutting you to pieces.
I'm shutting the door
to the kingdom in your face.
I'm paying you back with harm
for all the harm you've done.
I'm planning your disaster,
from which you cannot save yourself.

Dr. Jacqueline Lawrence

17known to pop up on our doorsteps without giving us any prior notice of their arrival, leaving us unprepared to accommodate them in the best possible manner- our restrooms may not be fresh, we may not have cold water in our refrigerator or time to sit and entertain them, or we may just not be in the mood for company. However, in the event of a family reunion, when out-of-town guests are expected, we are typically aware of, at a minimum, an estimated time of their arrival to our homes, and have the opportunity to be more adequately prepared- mentally, physically, emotionally, spiritually, and financially. Sometimes, on the other hand, even when we have been given ample notification of our guest's estimated time of arrival, because of our complacency, laziness, hectic schedules, apathy, unbelief that they will actually show up, and show up on time, and/or the division with members of our household, we fail to make suitable provisions for them.

Although Jesus, Himself, is unaware of the day and hour of His appearing (Mark 13:32), and even though He was not required to give us one clue about the time He would be coming for His family reunion with us, He graciously answered His disciple's questions of "When will these things happen and what will be the sign of the end of the age and of your coming?" He not only gave us a clear, estimated time of arrival by sharing ample signs of the perilous end times that would precede His coming, but also, solutions for us to prepare for, and endure them.

When we are expecting guests at our homes, we do not begin making preparations when we see them standing at the door and knocking, but we expect to have everything well-prepared for them at some point in time prior to their arrival. Likewise, when Jesus stands at the door, knocking, He expects us to be ready to swing it wide open. Because none of us knows exactly when He will return for us, we must make preparations for His coming now, so that we can be ready when He arrives, just like He warned us to be (Matthew 24:44). He did not say, "**GET** READY", but to eliminate all excuses, He commanded us to "**BE** READY". Of course, in order for us to be ready, we must first get ready, or prepare. Therefore, because we do not know the day or hour when we must **BE** READY, even though He gave us clear and ample signs of His coming, if we are not already ready, no matter how saved we are, we are not ready, and must **URGENTLY** make preparations for all the sorrows and woes that are unfolding right before our very eyes, even today.

Although, when preparing for family reunion guests to visit our homes, we do all we can to make our guests comfortable and "feel at home", still, there are some things for which we may not be able to prepare, as they are beyond our control; perhaps our money is low and we may not be able to purchase all the food we want to make available for them, maybe we had to work overtime that week and did not have time to straighten the cupboards or the garage, or shop for that new comforter set. Perhaps conceivably, our car might be on the brink and we may not be able to provide transportation for them, or there may have been a recent flood that soaked the carpet in our living room, making it inconvenient for everyone to live comfortably. We do all that we can to accommodate our guests according to our abilities and availabilities, and trust that God will do the rest.

At the time that our guests are expected to arrive, our goal is to be ready to receive them. We must therefore, keep track of time, so that we will remain on schedule in completing our tasks, so that when our company arrives, we can open wide our door for them with pride, because our house is in order. Even though, at the expected time of their arrival, we may be anticipating that our guests will knock on our door, we must be careful to guard it, and no matter how excited we might be about their arrival, prior to opening it, we must take precautions to peep through the peephole to make sure we are not opening our door to a thief or intruder. Just as members of our households come together to get our homes and ourselves ready for our out-of-town guests who have given us an estimated time of arrival, end time Christians must unite to prepare the household of faith for the coming of Christ, keeping track of time, protecting our household from intruders, and being faithful over our assignments so as one body, we will be ready.

CHAPTER 4

END TIME SOLUTIONS

With regard to the end times, not even Jesus knows the time of the end, but only the Father (Mark 13:32). I believe Jesus loves us, and wants us to survive the end time devastation so much, that being human, if He knew the exact day and hour of the end, He might have been tempted to abolish the secrecy of "When" the end would occur, by telling His disciples loudly and plainly. However, the Father saw fit to keep this piece of information a secret even from the Son, making us responsible for keeping watch and being ready at all times, remaining faithful doers of that which we have heard, alert, and prayerful. We must be careful not to be caught off guard, our hearts weighed down with sin, drunkenness, and the anxieties of life (Mark 13:13, 36, Luke 21:34). In these last days, we must grow up as mature Christians, renew our minds, rebuke the devourer, and lay aside every weight that has our hearts bound, so we can be free to be about our Father's business more now, than ever before.

We must obey God's commands so that we can live the abundant life that He has purposed for us. More than ever, as one people, we must love one another, humble ourselves, pray, and seek His face. More now than ever before, we must delight ourselves in God, feed the hungry, give drink to the thirsty, entertain the stranger, clothe the naked, care for the sick, and visit the imprisoned. As end time children of God, more now than ever before, we must teach the good news of Jesus Christ, baptize all nations, making disciples of them, unite, and remain free from sin and fear.

Jesus did not openly tell us everything we need to do in order for us to be ready for the end, but in telling us the signs of the things to come, with careful, and intentional study, it is not difficult for us to determine the various assignments that we need to accomplish in order for us to be prepared, based on the information He gave us. Even now, Christians all over the world should be praying to be able to escape all that is about to happen so we may be able to stand before the Son of Man. Being "able" implies that we will rely on our talents and intelligence to escape and stand, just as abolitionists of the Underground Railroad relied on their intelligence and skills to help runaway slaves escape and stand when they entered the Promised Land. Saints of God, therefore, are commanded to pray that our Father will give us the intelligence and skills necessary to escape the great tribulations of the end, and to stand victoriously when we see Jesus coming for us.

If Jesus expects us to stand when He returns, it is only logical that as devastating as the end times will be, He has provided several solutions- some openly, others, implied- for us to survive them. He made it clear that we should keep watch of the blossoming signs just as we would keep watch of the tenderness of the branches and the leaves of fig trees to know when summer is near (Mark 13:28-29). Figs being one of the most highly perishable fruit, just as the owner of fig trees would not wait until the figs are harvested to determine their uses, lest they over-ripen and cannot be eaten, we, too, must be ready for times of great tribulations before the harvest time, or the end (Matthew 13:39).

The inevitable and very pronounced first trimester signs of the end times which Jesus shared- mass deception, false Messiahs and prophets, wars and rumors of wars, national and kingdom divisions, natural disasters, famine, plagues, wickedness, hatred, familial betrayals, rebellion, persecution, imprisonment and murder of Christians, fearful events and great signs from heaven, spiritual complacency, terrors, sorrows, tribulations, and distresses- have been exponentially escalating in frequency and intensity from the beginning of time, and will continue, until the end. Many have predicted "the end" based on these signs, alone. However, Jesus assured us that these catastrophic events do not signify the end, but as the end draws nearer, they will continue to increase in strength and frequency, like birth pains.

Smooth talking, charismatic, money hungry, false Christs will appear, who will disgrace the Christian faith and say they are God. Because of their hate for Christians, these masters of deception will do all they can to trick children of God and cause them to turn away from the faith, just as satan used trickery in the Garden of Eden. They will persecute, imprison, and even kill Christians simply because they hate our status as children and heirs of God. Some of these individuals will be our very own friends and family members- our parents, brothers, sisters, relatives. Unfortunately, more and more, people are leaning strongly on, and taken captive through the lies, hollow and deceptive philosophies, and charming speech of greedy and false prophets who are masquerading as apostles of Christ while promoting shameful oppositions against the truth. They are eager to hear the dreams of psychics and other unspiritual spiritualists who depend on philosophy, vain deceit, human tradition, and worldly teachings, rather than on Christ (Colossians 2:8).

Concerning mass deceptions and false Messiahs and prophets, prominent signs of the end of the age, Jesus instructed us to stand firm in our faith so we will not be deceived by this lying breed, but so we will be saved (Matthew 24:4, 13). To them, we should not even lend our ear. We must be fully armored so that we will be able to stand against the devil's schemes, not one hair of our head, perishing (Ephesians 6:10-18, Luke 21:16-19). More now than ever, we must not believe every spirit, but test the spirits to see whether they acknowledge that Jesus Christ has come in the flesh, as this is how we know the spirit is from God (1 John 4:1-2). We should remain prayerful that we will not be deceived by those who will mislead us into thinking we will not reap the pits of hell by unrighteous living.

God will, and has, armed and appointed some of His children with the task of warning others about deceitful practices, schemes and individuals. Because some of us will be fugitives who will be captured and delivered to synagogues, or churches, to be imprisoned, it is implied that the churches and synagogues will be, and even now, are being, overtaken by our enemies. We will be brought before kings and governors all on account of Jesus' name, and will bear testimony to Him. Therefore, more and more, our nation is also being ran by politicians who are our adversaries. God told us not to worry beforehand about what we will say when we are arrested and brought to trial, but to say whatever is given us at the time by the Holy Ghost (Mark 13:11). We must believe that where we are weak, God is strong. He is our protector over all of our circumstances and if God is with us, no matter how powerful anyone else may be, it matters not who is against us- crooked pastors and priests, politicians, even the anti-Christ, himself- because we already have the victory if we test the spirits, remain fully armored and prayerful that we will stand firm until the end.

STAND FIRM UNTIL THE END

Blessed are we who do not fall away
on account of Jesus.
We, who hold firmly to the blessed hope we had at first,
are going to make it.
He'll keep us strong to the end,
so we'll be blameless on the day He calls us in.
So keep your mind clear and self-controlled,
so you can pray:

Lord, help us to stand firm 'til the end in this last hour.
Help us to stand our ground and take root in this last day.
When trouble and persecution comes,
help us to not drift away from you,
but to continue in our faith, being established and firm;
not moved from the hope of the gospel.
When we suffer, help us to not be ashamed
to praise you in Jesus' Name.

For many Godless deceivers
have secretly slipped in among us.
They are antichrists; rebellious men,
and man do they hate us!
They deny that Jesus came
from His Father in the flesh.
They change the grace of God
into a license for immorality.

Lord, help us to stand firm 'til the end in this last hour.
Help us to stand our ground and take root in this last day.
When trouble and persecution come,
help us to not drift away from you,
but to continue in our faith, being established and firm;
not moved from the hope of the gospel.
When we suffer, help us to not be ashamed
to praise you in Jesus' Name.

We are not in this battle alone, but God is always with us, and in Him, we will always be victorious. His Holy Spirit, who searches all things and reveals the deep things of God to us, intercedes through wordless groans. We must trust the God that we serve, that by His Spirit, He will speak through our mouths so that by His power, we will be victorious. He will teach us wise words of wisdom to say and bring the things Jesus told us to our remembrance so that none of our adversaries will be able to resist or contradict us (John 14:26, Luke 21:12-15). We, ourselves, are unable to do this in our own power, but by the power of the Most-High, who will overshadow us (Luke 1:35).

Wars and rumors of war have been, and will be, a major feature of human existence from the book of Genesis (Chapter 14:1-24) to the end of time. Some believe the world will end in nuclear war, but Jesus comforts us by letting us know that the end will not result in war. He told us not to be terrified when we hear of wars and rumors of wars (Luke 21:9). Because all must die, as Christians, we should not fear death, so if we must go into battle, then into battle we must go. God wants us to be strong, courageous, and faithful under all circumstances, even, and especially, when faced with death for His sake. Some saints will be commissioned by God to go to war and perhaps even lead kingdoms and nations to promote love, unity, and peace. Because both spiritual and natural warfare are inevitable, we must all position ourselves as soldiers of Christ and fight the good fight of faith, taking hold of the eternal life in which we professed in the presence of many witnesses, and to which we were called (1 Timothy 6:12).

As we get nearer and nearer to the end, the increase in frequency and intensity of natural disasters becomes undisputedly more pronounced. Earthquakes, hurricanes, global warming, tsunamis, drought, wild fires, floods, thunder, ice, snow, and hail storms, extreme heat, severe cold and frost, drought, volcano eruptions, avalanches, landslides, great signs from heaven, and disaster induced pestilences, famines, and wild fires are becoming more commonplace and evident in unforeseen places. Many say the exponential increase of natural disasters have intensified and become more frequent within the time span of their lifetime, alone. God will undoubtedly appoint some to teach, warn, and encourage others to prepare for the many increasing and impending natural disasters, famines, and diseases by growing fruit and vegetation, storing up food, water, clothing, emergency, medical, and other supplies, devising evacuation plans, establishing emergency shelters, and becoming scientists and skilled health care professionals to combat deadly diseases such as AIDS, heart disease, cancer, Ebola, and perhaps other perilous pestilences to come. As the first trimester terrors increase, however, even with increased solutions, more and more deaths will undoubtedly occur.

Because we have already been forewarned of these atrocities, God expects His children to be Ambassadors for Him, ready and positioned to properly handle them. To appropriately manage the many inevitable sorrows and deaths that will escalate more and more as we approach the end, in establishing His army, God will appoint some to sell fire, flood, earthquake, health, long-term care, life, funeral, and other types of insurance plans. Some must heed their call to become ministers, being sure to not only share the good news of the salvation of Jesus Christ and make disciples of God's children, but to prepare them for the devastations of the end times. Increasingly, if we take heed to Jesus' warnings, more and more children of God will be appropriately positioned to become morticians, Christian counselors, authors, gospel artists, social media bloggers, gardeners, canning and food preparers, survivalists/preppers, hunters, fishers, firearm trainers, emergency response members, owners and workers at homeless shelters and food ministries.

<u>The fulfillment of Jesus' command for us to go throughout all nations to make disciples of people- teaching His commandments, sharing His gospel,</u> and baptizing (Matthew 28:19-20), signifies the end, and is the line of demarcation that separates the first and second trimester birth pains. Because of the increase in travel and technology, the gospel is spreading faster and faster, thus, pushing us closer and closer to the end (Daniel 12:4). Logically speaking, it is our obedience to His Great Commission, then, that will birth the end. Therefore, the rational answer to Jesus' disciple's question of when the end will come, is when our work here on earth, is finished.

GO INTO ALL THE WORLD

Go into all the world and preach the good news to all creation.
Summon the people to the mountain of the temple of the Lord
so it can be established as chief among the mountains.
Raise up His Holy mountain above the hills
so that people will stream to it and offer sacrifices of righteousness,
bringing the grace of God's salvation for all men to see.

Invite everyone to share in the feast of the Lord, God Almighty-
a feast of rich food- the best of meat, the finest of aged wines.
Go and make disciples of all nations,
baptizing them in the name of the Father, Son, and Holy Spirit
so they can feast on the abundance of the seas
and the hidden treasures of the sand.

Although the harvest is plentiful, the workers are few,
but God will send workers out in His field if we ask Him to.
In order for His harvest to bear fruit and grow,
we must go into all the earth, like lambs among ferocious wolves,
preaching repentance and forgiveness of sin in His Name
to the ends of the world and to all nations.

For how can they believe in and call on Jesus, whom they have not heard?
We must share God's Word while we can;
the gospel that we heard, God's grace in all its truth;
the Good News that is being proclaimed to all creatures under heaven.
Show mercy, mixed with fear, and snatch them from the fire.
Hate even the stains on the clothing from their corrupted flesh.

Warn the wicked man; the least of them to the greatest!
Tell him if he does not turn from his wickedness
and from his evil ways, he will die for his sin.
Tell him the day is near;
there will be panic, not joy upon the mountains- a time of doom,
an unheard of disaster is coming, and that the end is coming soon.

The second trimester consists of the days of vengeance that all things written be fulfilled. This period is launched by Jerusalem being surrounded by armies and then the abominable anti-Christ positioning himself in the holy place (Matthew 24:14-15, Luke 21:20, 22). This period will be the worst in the history of mankind. In fact, it will be so horrific that it will be shortened so that even God's elect will be able to endure them (Matthew 24:21-22). Jesus reminded us in Matthew 24:15 about Daniel's prophesies that the anti-Christ, who will appear as an angel of light, will confirm a covenant with many for seven years. This seven-year period will be known as the tribulation period. Midway through, he will withdraw from his agreement. This latter three and a half years of the tribulation period is known as the great tribulation period.

During this period, the anti-Christ and his armed forces that have surrounded Jerusalem will rise up to blaspheme the temple. From the time that the daily sacrifice is abolished, and the abomination that causes desolation is set up, there will be 1,290 days. Those who wait for and reach the end of the 1,335 days, will be blessed (Daniel 9:27, 11:31, and 12:11-12 NIV). For 1,260 days, all hell will break loose until the power of God's people has been completely scattered (Daniel 12:7) and the abomination that causes desolation is eventually consumed with the spirit of the mouth, and destroyed by the brightness of the coming of Jesus (2 Thessalonians 2:8). According to Daniel 8:13-14, concerning the daily sacrifice, the rebellion that causes desolation, the surrender of the sanctuary and the trampling underfoot of the Lord's people, will take 2,300 days, and then the sanctuary will be re-consecrated.

Bible prophecy found in the book of Daniel concerning Daniel's visions about the end times have stumped bible prophecy scholars, and have added to the end time confusion and division for generations, as there are many differing opinions about the interpretations of times and dates (the evenings and mornings of Daniel, Chapter 8, and the weeks and years mentioned in Daniel, Chapter 9). However, if Daniel, God's esteemed prophet, who had understanding in all visions and dreams (Daniel 1:17), had to earnestly seek for the meaning of, and ultimately be made to understand, the vision concerning the end, and still did not understand it until he began praying, and then, later, slipped back into a lack of understanding (Daniel 12:8), saints of God must IMMEDIATELY stop all the arguments and debates and plead with God in prayer and petition, in fasting, and in sackcloth and ashes, for understanding. And after praying, we must believe that we, like Daniel, will either go our way, and get our rest until the end, or when the vision, which has been shut up, is opened, those who are wise will be given understanding of it at the appointed time of the end.

This abomination, or anti-Christ, spoken of by the prophet, Daniel, will speak against God. He will have full authority to deceive, oppress, persecute, wage war against, and destroy God's children. Powerful, but not by his own power, he will exalt himself over all, and those who exalt him, will he exalt over many. He will force all inhabitants of the earth to receive a mark on his right hand or on his forehead. In fact, He will be so vain, that he will claim to be God, and most likely, right at the point when children of God are close to agreeing- based on times and dates- that he is actually the anti-Christ, he will even attempt to change times and dates (Daniel 7:21, 25, 8:24, 11:36-39, 2 Thessalonians 2:4). Although it is God's will for us to escape all these things that will happen, many children of God will be beheaded and otherwise, destroyed. Because we know in advance that these things will happen, we must make plans in advance to escape the hell, distress, and destruction of the anti-Christ.

Those who are in Judea have been warned to take flight INTO the mountains so their pursuers would not find them (Matthew 24:16). We must understand that inhabitants of Judea who are referenced in this passage are followers of Christ which began with a group of people in Judea who were once under the power of the devil, but because Jesus healed them with the Holy Spirit and power, this group of believers has spread throughout the nations (Acts 10:36-38). Therefore, the reader of this passage of scripture must understand that all of those who are in the household of faith throughout the entire world must take flight.

Because the anti-Christ will have power over EVERYONE on the earth- world leaders, celebrities, professional athletes, black and white, rich and poor, male and female, fat and thin, old and young, Christians and atheists, straight and gay- as we get closer and closer to the end, the world will be getting closer and closer to becoming a one world government with one form of money, one set of rules and liberties, and one religion for all. Although, as Christians, we may utilize all our power to prevent this one world government from going into effect, because the bible told us in advance that it, as well as all other end time signs, is inevitable, we should be doing all we can to prepare for it. We should not allow ourselves to be tricked by promises of peace and safety in exchange for this Global World Order, as it will only lead to our destruction (1 Thessalonians 5:3).

Jesus never mentioned this new world order, but if the world will be controlled by this one man of lawlessness, then it will become a lawless world. We must pray that we would be able to escape all the lawlessness and catastrophes that will occur during the three-and-a-half year period from the time Jerusalem is surrounded by armies and the anti-Christ steps in to the holy temple and proclaims to be the Messiah, to the Second Coming of Jesus Christ. We must keep watch of these signs so that we will know when to be ready to evacuate, taking flight into the mountains, as only pure hell will be left behind! It is not a part of God's plan for all of us to endure the sufferings inflicted by the abomination that causes desolation, in fact, in the seventh Chapter of Revelation, we learn that great multitudes who have washed their robes white in the blood of the Lamb, will come out of the great tribulation to stand at the throne of God. Because we know this, our plans will, in no uncertain terms, coincide with God's plans. However, in order for great tribulation saints to stand at the throne of God, they must, and they will flee from the sword, famine and plagues of the city with haste, without passing go or collecting $200.00, and without looking back or returning to their homes or inside the city to get anything- cell phones, purses, hats, jackets, food, water, computers, bibles, or money!

DON'T LOOK BACK

When rebels have become completely wicked,
make sure your bags are completely packed and hidden.
When the wicked rise to power,
take your mark and get set to not look back.

When that stern-faced king arises,
run as fast as you can and flee to the mountains.
When He's standing strong, but not by his own power,
make sure you're well hidden, and don't you dare look back.

When he starts causing astounding devastations,
you should have already come out from amongst them.
When he succeeds in everything he does,
hopefully your eyes are kept to the hills and you won't look back.

When he destroys mighty men and the holy people,
hide yourself and your loved ones even deeper.
When the master of intrigue causes deceit to prosper,
forget about the things you lack and please don't look back.

When folk start to feel at peace and secure,
know that your redemption is drawing near.
When he takes his stand against the Prince of princes,
keep watch of the clouds if they are in sight and don't look back.

When he considers himself superior,
God's Word hid in your heart, keep your mind on the Savior.
When he is destroyed, but not by human power,
you'll soon see the Messiah coming with His angels, so don't look back.

Prayerfully, children of God will be delivered from seeing the horror of this day that will be so devastating that people will be crying with grief and mourning in all the streets and highways (Amos 5:16). Violence, murder, rape, and looting will be commonplace. People will be desperately in need of help, but few will be there to help them. The whole world will be turned upside down. During this devastating period of great tribulation, there will not only be a spiritual famine, but a natural famine in the land that will be so great that the barren woman will be considered blessed because she, unlike the pregnant woman and the woman with children, will not be put in a position to make the decision to eat her own starving children (Luke 23:29, Deuteronomy 28:53)

BLESSED, BARREN WOMAN

Blessed, barren woman
whose wombs have never bore, and whose breasts have never nursed.
How awful the suffering will be on that day the enemy inflicts;
none will be like it, and none has ever been.
It will be a time of distress and disaster that causes the ear to tingle,
so sing, oh barren woman!

Blessed, barren woman!
You have no fruit of your womb, no flesh of children to eat,
no thirst of an infant's tongue to quench, no hunger to curb,
no milk in your breasts to even consider nursing your young,
no little ones dashed to the ground while your belly is ripped open.
Shout for joy, oh barren woman!

Blessed, barren woman
who never bore a child and have never been in labor,
but has given birth to more children than of her who has a husband.
Our Father opens your womb and delivers you from times of trouble.
He settles you in your home as a happy mother of children.
So sing and shout for joy, oh barren woman!

Just as an "on call" airline pilot, exhausted from working six consecutive days of double shifts, might pray that he would not be awakened from his sleep by a call to report to work in hostile, winter weather conditions, this prophetic flight to the mountains for great tribulation, heavenly bound saints, could potentially be so devastating, that Jesus warned us to start praying in advance that it will not take place in the winter, or on the Sabbath, when we are most in need of rest (Matthew 24:20-21). Very few even concern themselves with the impending distress for those who will be left behind, let alone, pray for their smooth flight. Even though some of us may escape the great tribulations of the end times by either being asleep in our graves or, as some believe, caught up in the air with our Lord, we must love God's great tribulation sheep enough to not only start praying for their safety, but also preparing for their safety, protection, and survival, now.

Even if believers make it safely to prepared hiding places into the mountains, just as bounty hunters pursued runaway slaves during the days of the enslavement of Africans, who, unfortunately, typically took flight during winter rains, storms, and snow in order to keep bloodhounds off their tracks, representatives of the anti-Christ's army will continue to attempt to hunt down children of God. They will use all types of deceptive tactics to trap them. Jesus forewarned us not to believe or follow false Christs when we hear them tell us to come out of hiding, and that He has already come, as if screaming to those hiding during a game of hide-and-seek, "Ally ally all come free! Come out, come out, wherever you are!" (Matthew 24: 23-27, Luke 21: 8). Following false Christs is a death trap! Once in hiding, no matter how anxious to see Jesus, tired of being cooped up in limited spaces, or inconvenienced by the lack of a comfortable home, neither children of God, nor their livestock, must go out to the fields or walk on the road, for the enemy has a sword, and there is fear on every side (Jeremiah 6:25). Jesus warned us not to be deceived, and assured us that when He returns, every eye will see Him- even those who pierced Him, the dead, as well as the living; even those who are blind, I am sure (Revelation 1:7).

So, when Jerusalem is being surrounded by armies and the anti-Christ stands in the holy place, we must understand that once those who are left behind obediently flee to the mountains, whether they are hiding from the conspiracy of the wicked in deep caves, holes in the ground, elaborate underground shelters, bunkers, strongholds, fields, deserts, vineyards, secret rooms, wildernesses, dry stream beds, among rocks and supplies, on mountain tops or clefts, or even at the bottom of the sea, they must remain in hiding until Jesus returns. God, whose eyes are constantly watching us, will make sure their eyes see Him, upon His return, and we will never need to be told He has come. We are therefore warned not to be deceived by anyone who tells us Jesus has already come, or to surface from our hiding places in order to see Jesus, as it will NEVER be true. Although our limited understanding may not fathom how every eye will see Him, everything is not meant for our understanding. If God's ways and thoughts were the same as ours, we would not need Him as our God. Just as sure as lightning flashes from one end of the sky to the other, those left behind must believe- but not necessarily, understand- that EVERY EYE will, in fact, see Jesus for themselves no matter where they are hiding, so STAY PUT!

SEE?

You cannot see Him.
He is not running around.
He is neither here nor there.
When He comes, He will not be anywhere
where we cannot all see Him.
So, do not be fooled when you think you see what you do
not see.
You see?

You cannot see Him.
That is not Him; he just wants you to think he is Him.
Do not believe his wondrous signs and miracles;
for as sure as lightning- being visible-
flashes and lights up the sky from the east to the west,
so will the coming of the Son of Man be.
You see?

When Jesus appears on the clouds of the sky
with power and great glory,
all of the nations will mourn when they see Him coming.
Then, with a loud trumpet call, He will send His angels
to weed out His kingdom from everything sinful and from
all who do evil.
The time is near when many will long to see Him, but will
not see.
You see?

The sun will be darkened.
The moon will not give its light.
The stars will fall down from the sky,
and the heavenly bodies will be shaken.
He will come with all power,
with great thunder and lightening
and He will be there, standing in His glory-
for all to see.
You see?

CHAPTER 5

STEAL AWAY

Because what has been, will be again, and what has been done will be done again, as there is nothing new under the sun (Ecclesiastes 1:9), just as the day finally came for Moses to lead the Israelites out of Egypt, and for some of the African slaves in the Americas to take flight to freedom from the atrocities of slavery, the day is coming when Christians all over the world will take flight to the wilderness through rough terrain, to get out of the reach of their enemy. Just as the Hebrew and African slaves were oppressed, persecuted, and murdered, Christians all over the world will become enslaved by the anti-Christ and his army because of their testimony about Jesus and because of the word of God (Revelation 6:9). Most of us are familiar with the story of how God told Moses to raise his staff so that He could part the Red Sea for all the Israelites to pass through, but how the seas covered and drowned the Egyptians who followed behind them. Just as God guided Moses to lead the Israelites out of the reach of the Egyptians, He guided white abolitionists such as John Brown, Peg Leg Joe, Levi Coffin, and free and/or fugitive slaves, such as Josiah Henson, Frederick Douglass, and Harriet Tubman (who, herself, is often referred to as the "Moses" of her people) to raise the staff known as The Underground Railroad to set captives free. And just as God was with Moses and Harriet during their flight to freedom, so will He be with Christians during times of great tribulation (Joshua 1:5).

The Underground Railroad, a network of people, safe houses, and escape routes required much work and the cooperation of many well-meaning, caring individuals. Operated in the United States of America in the early to mid-1800s by both blacks and whites who loved God's sheep enough to feed and take care of them, The Underground Railroad was a figurative and secretive evacuation plan patterned after a railroad, its purpose, to help black runaway slaves of the south find their way up north to Canada where they could be free. Abolitionists established shelters for the fugitives, which could usually be identified by a display of quilts, lit lamps inside the homes, and white bricks on top of chimneys. Slaves were hidden in barns, cabinets, cellars, closets, attics, basements, false walls, trap doors, tunnels, and crawl spaces at the homes of abolitionists, where they would be fed, provided medical care, and otherwise taken care of along their journey; prayerfully, of no return.

Fortunately, not only would abolitionists pack provisions for the slaves' journey, sometimes they would hide food, water, blankets and clothing in caves and mountains for their comfort. For the most part, however, running away to the north was anything but comfortable. Slaves usually traveled long treks through the wilderness, mostly by foot, and at night, through swamps, caves, thorns, thistles, and rivers. Occasionally, they were transported from one location to the next, which obviously had to be done under the most secretive conditions. The first step was to flee from the control of the slaveholder, or master. For many slaves, this meant relying on their own very limited resources- perhaps an extra dress or pair of pants, a blanket, a tool, and very little food. Some food, such as wild berries and small game, was available along their journey, however, many starved to death. Because of the dangerous conditions, many slaves also died from harsh weather conditions, or were killed by wild animals. Countless slaves were caught by slave catchers and were either killed, sold to new slave owners, or returned to their masters.

Although the slaves on the plantations may have heard of The Underground Railroad, and may have known that its appearance was near, for the most part, they never knew the exact day or hour when abolitionists would be coming through, so they had to keep watch and be ready to take flight at all times, remaining alert and on guard, with their bags packed and well hidden, typically in some remote location. They most likely prayed that their flight would not take place in the winter or on the Sabbath, that they would be able to escape the horrific consequences that would potentially be associated with their journey, and most importantly, that they would be able to stand when they arrived to Canada, the Promised Land.

Although the Underground Railroad system had nothing to do with an actual and physical underground railroad, or with railroading at all, for that matter, those involved with this organization aimed at guiding runaway slaves to safety, found it necessary to protect its secretiveness, and therefore, spoke a TOP SECRET language when referring to its operation. Due to the fact that railroads were a common mode of transportation used back in the 1800s, just as airlines are, today, and since slaves were transported from one destination to another, as in the railroad industry, and because of the secretiveness of the operation, the term, "Underground Railroad", was birthed.

The secretive language used to conceal the operation of the Underground Railroad consisted of terms related to the railroad industry. "Conductors", for example, moved freight (runaway slaves), also known as packages, or baggage, from one station to the next, typically by foot, in shipping boxes, boats, or wagons with false bottoms, for purposes of camouflaging hiding spaces. "Stations", also known as "safe houses", where fugitives would rest, eat, and wait for their next piece of instruction for taking flight to their subsequent safe house, which was typically 10 to 20 miles away, were managed by "station masters" in their homes and businesses. Business stations were entire buildings or structures, and not individual rooms or parts of larger structures. Goods, such as money, clothing, food, coats, and blankets contributed by "shareholders", who were comprised of individuals, churches and other ministries and organizations, were stored in business stations. Escape routes from station to station, were called "lines".

The slaves on the plantations sang songs to make the work day go by faster. Many of the songs were of a spiritual nature and were sung to reveal coded and secretive messages- even within earshot of the plantation master. The song, "Go Down, Moses" exposed the slave's strong urge and unwavering determination to be set free. "Follow The Drinking Gourd" instructed the slaves to follow the North Star to freedom. "Swing Low, Sweet Chariot" and "The Gospel Train" informed the slaves that their opportunity for freedom was soon approaching through the Underground Railroad. "Wade in the Water" warned the slaves to cross the river or enter the water to deter the bloodhounds from their tracks. One very popular song was "Steal Away", which had several coded meanings. The obvious intent of the song was to reveal the need for people to flee from the bondage of sin and become freed by the blood of Jesus, and thus, slaves to God, so that once they face their inevitable death, their spirits will inescapably steal away home to Jesus. Secret codes of the song symbolized the slave's yearning for freedom from the bondage of slavery, and the need for family and friends to be ready for an upcoming flight northward, to make plans for an imminent, secret meeting in the woods at night to prepare for an oncoming freedom flight, and/or to carve out a special time for prayer and worship.

STEAL AWAY

Steal away, steal away, steal away to Jesus!
Steal away, steal away home,
I ain't got long to stay here.

My Lord, He calls me,
He calls me by the thunder;
The trumpet sounds within my soul,
I ain't got long to stay here.

Green trees are bending,
Poor sinners stand a-trembling;
The trumpet sounds within my soul,
I ain't got long to stay here.

My Lord, He calls me,
He calls me by the lightning;
The trumpet sounds within my soul,
I ain't got long to stay here.

By Wallace Willis

The mission of the Underground Railroad was accomplished because of the brotherly love, unity, and organization of caring individuals who were determined to steal away for prayer and to make plans for fugitives to steal away to freedom. Just as God spoke into existence the plan of the Underground Railroad, He also spoke into existence a plan for His wise and faithful servants to steal away to build up the highway called "The way of holiness" (Isaiah 35:8). Like the Underground Railroad, during the days of black slavery in America, The way of holiness, too, requires unity, cooperation, wisdom, faithfulness, and hard work for the success of its operation. Therefore, children of God must help our brothers and sisters at the proper time, which, because no man knows the day or hour when our mass flight will take place, is NOW!

If a top secret organization similar to the Underground Railroad were established today to feed, take care of, and set the captives free- out of the reach of their enemy- during times of great tribulation, because airplanes are a more common mode of transportation, an "Underground Airline", would most likely be established. Unlike the black slaves who were accustomed to living in sub-standard conditions, many today are adjusted to a higher standard of living, and therefore, if abolitionist stockholders were generous enough to donate supplies for passengers today, there would probably be a laundry list of desired items, such as canned, and other non-perishable food, seeds, tools, water, clothing, diapers, medicine, underground bunkers, beds, toilets, tents, generators, flashlights, batteries, blankets, cell phones, computers, first aid kits and other emergency and medical supplies and, undoubtedly, luxury items commonly used today.

If abolitionists could pull together during the days of African slavery in the United States by helping as many as 100,000 people to escape northward to freedom in only forty, short years, with today's sophistication of modern technology; books and e-books, the internet, television, a variety of transportation services, including, but not limited to airplanes, jets, trucks, buses, boats, recreational, and other vehicles, newspapers, telephones, fax machines, satellites, radio and the like, imagine how many more people, in even much less time, we could save today if, as one people, we would raise a staff to build up the highway.

CHAPTER 6

WHO THEN?

After warning His disciples about the signs of the end of the age and of His coming, Jesus turned the tables and asked them a very profound, question, as if saying, "Now that you know what the signs are, and as much as I have shared with you about when these things will happen, which of you are going to do something about that which you have heard?", by inquiring, "Who then is a faithful and wise servant, whom his Lord hath made ruler over his household, to give them meat in due season (Matthew 24:45-47)?" Surely, this question was meant to be literal, and not rhetorical, still standing firm today. So, who, then? God is expecting us to love His sheep enough to feed and take care of them, not only now, but also, during times of great tribulations. So, again, WHO THEN?

Those who will be left behind to endure this period of sorrow and suffering have been commanded to take flight on a three-and-a-half-year journey of no return (Daniel 12). They will be unable to buy or sell anything unless they take the mark of the beast- 666- which, if they take it, will lead them straight to the pits of hell (Revelation 13:17-18). No one, not even Jesus, knows when this international flight is scheduled for take-off. Therefore, it only makes sense that, like the abolitionists in the days of the Underground Railroad, believers establish an underground network of adequately equipped safe houses, escape routes, and transportation services, so that when the proper time comes for this mass evacuation, places of safety and provision will already be prepared for them, and passengers will be able to stand in victory when they see the Son of Man come to take them to heaven, their final destination. (Let the reader understand).

During this period of great tribulation- from the time the anti-Christ sets up his image in the holy place- many countries will fall, but Edom, Moab and the chief of the children of Ammon will be supernaturally delivered from his hand (Daniel 11:41). These kingdoms on the west side of Israel known as Jordan, will be under divine protection from God. He will give them two wings of a great eagle, that she might fly into the wilderness, into her place, where she is nourished for a time, and times, and half a time, from the face of the serpent (Revelation 12:14). God will build a highway for those from Edom, Moab and the chief of the children of Ammon who walk on that way called The way of holiness (Isaiah 35:8), and will send His angel to guard them and lead them to safety- out of harm's reach of satan, wild animals, and the desert heat, to a land flowing with milk, honey, and riches stored in secret places.

The anti-Christ hates us so much that destroying us will be heavy on his mind. He, and those with his spirit and who do not acknowledge Jesus (1 John 4:1-3), will heavily pursue children of God. They will be swifter than eagles, chasing them over mountains, and secretly lying in wait for them in the wilderness (Lamentations 4:19). They will surround them (Luke 19:43) and do everything they can to lure them out of the mountains- setting traps on the ground to capture them when they think they will come out to get food. God, therefore, expects us to emulate for the rest of the saints of the world in the natural, what He will do for those in the western region of Jordan, in the supernatural. He expects us to understand that when this international flight takes off, airports into the mountains must already be operational and fully stocked with food, water, bedding, clothing, generators, medical, and other necessary supplies, planes must be fully equipped to transport passengers down cleared runways called the way of holiness, and pilots, stewardesses, baggage handlers, ticket agents and other key personnel must be in place.

Therefore, just as Joseph collected and stored up huge quantities of food in the good years, and as ants of little strength store up their food in the summer, we, too, must bring the whole tithe into the storehouse, along with our increased offerings, so that there will be meat in God's house (Malachi 3:10), and so that God will increase our store of seed. We must prepare the way in the wilderness so that saints of God can be led to safety. We must develop runways, turning mountains into roads, raising up highways by filling in valleys, lowering every mountain and hill, straightening crooked roads, and smoothing out rough ways. To provide direction to our pilots, we must clearly mark our runways, setting up road signs, putting up guideposts, and lifting up banners. Once the highway has been developed and marked, we must take note of the highway, creating flight plans (Luke 3:5-6, Jeremiah 31:21 NIV).

Unfortunately, some selfish-minded believers do not think they will personally be affected by the devastations to come. Believing they will either be dead or caught up in the air with Jesus, even if they knew what it meant to be ready, they do not feel it is necessary for them to do anything to prepare for the end times, as long as they are saved. Others are convinced that if they are alive during the great tribulation period, God will deliver them from the hand of the anti-Christ as He will do for those in Edom, Moab, and the leaders of Ammon. However, God did not say He would rescue them, but instead, said that many countries will fall. Still, others have resigned to being beheaded, should it become required, as it may. However, above all else, it is God's desire that we prosper and be in health, even as our souls prosper- even until the end (3 John 1:2). Therefore, we must plan to live, but be prepared to die.

Whether we are dead, raptured, or otherwise delivered from the hand of the anti-Christ, if our former "fence-straddling" and unbelieving brothers and sisters who will be purified, made spotless, and refined, are left behind to suffer the devastation of the great tribulation period- some of whom, may be our very own loved ones, and perhaps, as much as we would not desire for it to happen, even ourselves- then as loving Christians, we should all be moved to help them. If God's great tribulation sheep are standing when Jesus returns, whether or not we are the ones who are left behind, then we are all standing, as one body. Therefore, as one body, we should all love God and His great tribulation sheep enough to unite and give them their food at the proper time, as this is God's will, and is what will please Him, immensely.

SHEEP FOOD

Here's some food that I want you to taste.
It came straight from heaven. Don't let it go to waste.
Taste this sweet bread of heaven, the body of Christ.
Have faith to believe He paid the price.
The Lamb of God told me, "Feed my sheep"
so that at the last day they won't have to weep.
I'm feeding you because He told me to,
and because I love Him, and I love you, too.

Here's some food that I want you to eat.
Let it fill up your spirit, so that you'll be complete.
Savor every word He gave us, let them enter your heart.
Purge all of your sins and take a brand new start.
God said if I love Him, I must feed you
until He comes back when this old world is through.
I'm feeding you because He told me to,
and because I love Him, and I love you, too.

Immediately following the horrific, second trimester labor pains, which will feature the empowerment of the anti-Christ, God will press the hypothetical power button, turning off the whole heaven and earth like an old, tired, worn-out, irreparably damaged machine. First, all the lights will go out (the sun, moon, and stars). Then will come the sputtering, rumbling, growling and roaring of a great earthquake that will shake the whole heaven and earth and toss all the seas (Matthew 24:29). Afterwards, that moment in history that we have all been waiting for will finally arrive; our family reunion with our Brother, Lord, and Savior, Jesus Christ. He will appear with great power and glory to command His angels to gather together from the ends of the earth to the ends of heaven (Mark 13:26-27), those of us who gave drink to the thirsty, hospitality to the stranger, clothes to the needy, care for the sick, visitations to the imprisoned, and food to the hungry.

FEED HIS SHEEP

Serve the people of God their food.
Give them all plenty to eat;
not just breast milk or baby food,
but graduate them to meat.

Keep them well-nourished so they can be strong
in their day of strife and trouble.
Make them aware that for all of their work,
their rewards will be doubled.

Give them their food at the proper time,
for Jesus is coming soon.
Help them to stand tall on the day
when the light leaves the sun, stars, and moon.

God commanded that we feed His sheep
who dwell in the caves and mountains
and give them plenty of water to drink
from His free-flowing fountain.

Be wise and faithful to these prophetic words.
Do not allow your faith to bend.
Keep watch and be ready, my brothers and sisters,
and stand firm until the end!

CHAPTER 7
PREPARING FOR TAKE-OFF

Because we are quickly approaching the end, we anticipate that only a few years will pass before great tribulation saints must embark on their journey of no return. Therefore, our Administrator, who is the Holy Spirit, has appointed Christians all over the world to establish an Airline Ministry which serves to fly great tribulation saints on two wings of a great eagle to a place prepared for them in the wilderness, where they would be taken care of for a time, times and half a time, out of the serpent's reach until their eyes see their Redeemer returning for them in the clouds (Revelation 12:14). Although we cannot guarantee the exact day or hour (Matthew 24:36) of our flight's take-off, most of us would agree that we are right on the verge of the fulfillment of Jesus' Great Commission for us to preach the gospel to all nations, and thus, of Jerusalem being surrounded by armies and the anti-Christ stepping in to the holy place.

Because we will never again see yesterday, now is the time, and prayerfully, not past the time, for us to fulfill God's evacuation plan that He did not find necessary to make known to people of earlier generations because of its irrelevance for their day (Ephesians 3:5). All Christians (including skilled professionals- electricians, plumbers, architects, carpenters, pilots, military personnel, social media specialists, security officers, medical practitioners, etc.) and Christian ministries (food, clothing, housing, etc.) must now unite to establish God's TOP SECRET, underground airline, for which He has provided the pattern through the Underground Railroad, the airline industry, Noah, Joseph, Lot, Moses, and many others.

Like Moses, who loved his people enough to prepare them for entering the Promised Land, but never entered himself, some Airport Managers may begin the process of establishing their airports, but for one reason or another, they may not complete and/or manage the operations, and therefore, will need a strong support team. It is of the utmost urgency that we begin building up the highway now, and ask God to give us grace to ascertain its completion before tragedy of the great tribulation period strikes. Because of terrorist pursuits to murder, imprison, and put to death the saints of God, flights are expected to be uncomfortable, as there will be strong turbulence along the way. However, the primary concern of this network of underground airports for end time believers, like the Underground Railroad, is for the safety and survival of its passengers.

Because of their love for children of God, Airport Managers are passionately dedicated to providing efficient and effective aviation services for their established, domestic or international airports, runways, and aircraft for their passengers. Much independent study is devoted to every aspect of their mission. However, to assist those whom God has called to become Airport Managers with their selfless tasks, for which they will be greatly rewarded, below are basic aviation guidelines used for lifting up a standard for the establishment and operation of independent airports. These guidelines have been summarized from the Federal Aviation Administration of the United States of America, from which additional information may be obtained. To effectively make plans for building up the highway so that great tribulation captives may be set free- out of the serpent's reach- as one people speaking the same language, Airport Managers and their volunteer personnel must first familiarize themselves with common key words and phrases used in the airline industry:

Aircraft

Airplanes, jets, helicopters, gliders, sea planes, hot air balloons, and a variety of other vehicle types used to transport passengers and cargos to various airports. Food, drink, emergency, and other supplies are typically available on airplanes.

Airstrip/Airfield

A kind of airport consisting only of a runway and fuel

Airport

Places of safety and temporary refuge that can range from a single gate area to multi-terminal mazes where passengers wait for flight arrivals and departures and cargo and luggage are loaded and unloaded. Airports consist of at least one surface, such as a runway for takeoffs and landings, and often include terminal buildings and aircraft storage. Larger airports have air traffic control, passenger facilities such as restaurants and lounges, and emergency services. Just as secret airplanes exist, secret airports established by secret agencies, also exist.

Airport Maps

Show the interior and exterior of airports, including, but not limited to: locations of all runways, markings, taxiways, ramps, parking areas, access roads, buildings, landsides, airsides, watch towers, management offices, concourses/terminals, vehicle storage, waste management areas, medical facilities, restaurants, lounges, restrooms, fire extinguishers, smoke detectors, storages, etc..

Air Traffic Control/Controllers

Persons designated to provide information to pilots and airports regarding weather conditions, traffic reports, aircraft clearances for take-offs and landings, essential ground and flight information, necessary holding patterns, and other perceived dangers

*See Air Traffic Controller Job Description

Air Traffic Control Tower

The name of the airport structure, that may be manned or unmanned by Air Traffic Controllers, which generally rises high above other buildings at an airport to give Air Traffic Controllers a view of aircraft moving on the ground and in the air around the airport.

Baggage Handler

Marshals the aircraft in the gate, loads, unloads, and sorts cargo and baggage

*See Baggage Handler Job Description

Boarding Pass

Delegates seat assignments on airplanes

Cargo

Food and supplies

Final Approach

A common term for landing an aircraft at the end of a flight

Final Destination

Final airport of arrival

Flight Attendant

The keeper of an airplane who ensures the security, safety and comfort of passengers

*See Flight Attendant Job Description

Flight Number

A number assigned to a designated flight

Flight Plan

Route and flying altitude

Gates

The physical areas of the airport where flights depart and arrive

"Holding Pattern"

When Air Traffic Control commands the pilot to turn away from the airport and remain circling in a designated pattern over the destination or alternate airport at an assigned altitude in the event of unexpected weather, congestion, or other danger at the airport, until further instructions are provided. The use of additional fuel is needed in the event holding is included in the flight plan, or becomes necessary to be added to the flight plan.

Itinerary

A list of flights that a passenger is scheduled to take

Landing

The last part of a flight where a flying airplane returns to the ground

Layover

Usually an overnight stop during the flight portion of a trip involving a change of airplanes or another form of transportation

Markings

Standardized lighting and ground markings usually found on larger runways to provide direction and identification to all air and ground crews.

Mechanic

Airport personnel that keep the planes operating safely and efficiently by servicing, repairing, overhauling, and testing aircraft

*See Aircraft Mechanic Job Description

Non-Stop Flight

A flight that does not stop at another airport before reaching its point of arrival

Passenger

One who flies on an airplane

Plane Spotters

Enthusiasts who spot secret planes

Pilot

One who transports passengers

*See Pilot Job Description

Red Eye

An overnight flight that arrives early the following morning

Runway

Area which the flight will "take-off" and land. Smaller or less-developed airports — which represent the vast majority — often have a single, shorter runway with dirt, grass, or gravel, whereas larger airports generally have paved, and longer runways.

Standby

The procedure of waiting for a seat to open up on a flight on which a passenger is not booked/confirmed

Stockholder

Donor of money, clothing, food and supplies for establishing and operating airlines

Stopover

A planned stop of at least one night (or more than 4 hours domestically), and then continuing the next part of a flight itinerary

"Take-off"

When an aircraft begins by taxiing on a runway, and then flies in the air

Taxiing

The movement of an aircraft on the ground

"The wind blows from the south today"

Warning of Plane Spotters nearby

Ticket

A contractual travel document between a traveler and an airline

Ticket Agent

Issuers of tickets who are responsible for assisting passengers with their travel needs

*See Ticket Agent Job Description

AIRPORT MANAGEMENT

All things decent and in order, each Airport Manager appoints the following support volunteers to assist in the establishment and operation of airports in accordance with the lines of responsibility in the graphic below.

Management Team Members efficiently and effectively establish and operate the airports. This particular Christian Airline Ministry requires that Airport Managers designate eleven trustworthy Management Team Members, for a total of twelve (12), which is a perfect number, signifying governmental perfection. Due to the fact that it is uncertain which Management Team Members, if any, will be left behind to operate the

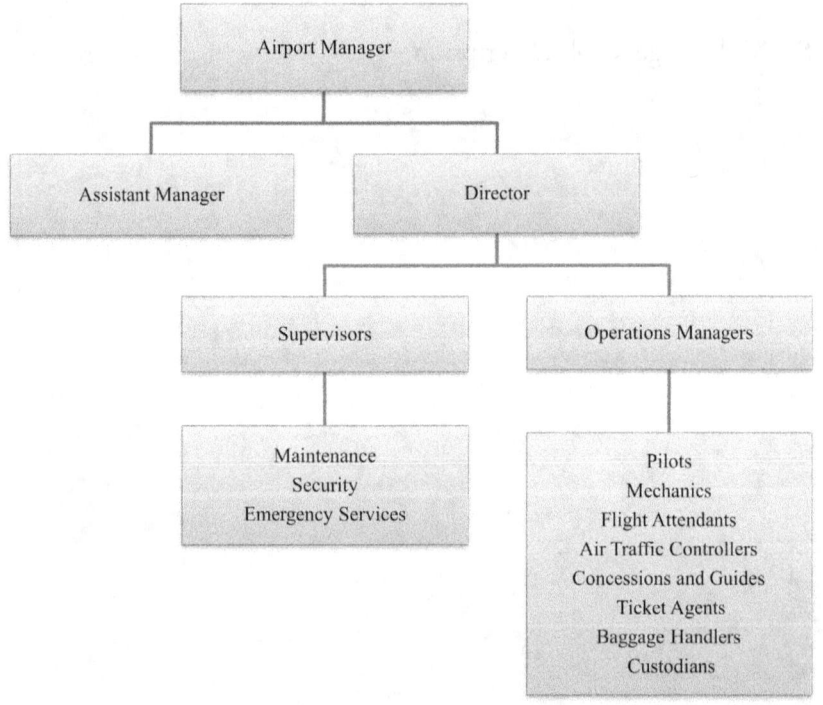

airline at the time of flight take-off, all Management Team Members, and perhaps others, must be trained to carry out the operations of the airport. Because it will typically take several years for an airport to fully function- from planning to operations- for the purpose of continuity and in the event of termination, death or perhaps even rapturing of any Management Team Members, it is imperative that Airport Managers not only complete all necessary written reports and maintain them in fire and water proof safes, to be maintained in secure and confidential locations of which all Management Team Members (and perhaps others) are aware, but Airport Managers must also maintain a list of an adequate number of alternate Management Team Members, including that of the Airport Manager.

Airport Managers are divinely appointed, voluntary servants of God who are responsible for the direct administration, operation, maintenance and management of established airports. Duties of the Airport Managers include, but are not limited to:

- Managing the financial aspects of running the airport
- Securing suitable airplanes
- Airport safety
- Planning and booking trips
- Securing adequate fuel supply
- Recruiting, appointing, and training a wise and faithful Management Team
- Installing ticket and boarding pass procedures
- Devising flight plan records

- Researching and networking with Airport Managers of other airports to share ideas about effectively planning, developing, and operating airports

- Researching and implementing vital information to increase the effectiveness of operations

- Reviewing plans with the Management Team, including Flight Plans and the Wildlife Management Plan, which is developed to alleviate the serious threats posed by wildlife when the same airspace and pavement is shared with aircraft

- Establishing a warning system to make all passengers aware of flight take-offs

<u>Airport Assistant Managers</u> assist Airport Managers with the fulfillment of all tasks and responsibilities of planning, establishing, and operating the airport. Tasks include, but are not limited to: purchases, maintenance, and securing aircraft, airports, vehicles, and equipment. Assistant Managers must be knowledgeable of everything concerning the airport of which the Managers are aware, and are typically the ones who steps in when the Airport Managers are no longer able to fulfill their duties.

<u>Airport Directors</u> are ultimately responsible for all airport policies and procedures, including but not limited to project management, staffing, and general operations. Airport Directors directly manage Airport Supervisors and Operations Managers.

<u>Airport Supervisors</u> are responsible for recruiting, training, and supervising security, maintenance, and emergency services. As such, it is the responsibility of Airport Supervisors to appoint and instruct support

staff to ascertain the efficient maintenance of the facilities and equipment and provision of security and emergency services, including, but not limited to inspection of airport premises for safety and fire hazards, maintenance and repair of fire and other equipment, and the coordination of assignments of emergency duties.

<u>Airport Operations Managers</u> are responsible for recruiting, training, and supervising qualified operations personnel, including but not necessarily limited to: Pilots, Mechanics, Flight Attendants, Baggage Handlers, Concessions, Guides, Custodians, Ticket Agents, and Air Traffic Controllers.

AVIATION JOBS

<u>Pilots</u> fly passengers and cargo to various airports in accordance with the information contained in Flight Plans for each individual flight. The aircraft is usually operated by two, three or four pilots, depending on the type of aircraft and length of the journey. The captain is the pilot-in-command, and has the overall responsibility for the safe and efficient operation of the aircraft, including its crew.

<u>Aircraft Mechanics</u> keep planes operating safely and efficiently. Mechanics service, repair, overhaul, and test aircraft.

<u>Air Traffic Controllers</u> control air traffic to ensure flight safety according to established procedures and policies by coordinating searches for missing aircraft, alerting emergency services when aircraft are experiencing difficulties, checking conditions and traffic at different altitudes in response to pilots' requests for altitude changes, and directing ground traffic and pilots to runways when safe.

<u>Flight Attendants</u> oversee the customer service aspects on airplanes, providing security, safety, and service to those on board. They are in continuous contact with the public, and must possess the ability to handle difficult situations, ranging from distressed and fearful passengers to unaccompanied children. They must provide assistance, leadership, and direction in accordance with all emergency situations, including, but not limited to, accidents, bomb threats, terrorism, or hijacking, while remaining calm.

<u>Baggage Handlers</u> expediently transfers baggage, equipment and supplies to aircraft, maintains safety and security of the ramp at all times, monitors customer safety during boarding and deplaning, assists

customers in a friendly and courteous manner, and services aircraft as needed (lavatories, portable water, window wash, and de-icing and commissary items).

Ticket Agents provide free tickets at airports or other locations, assign seats for passengers, if applicable, and re-book passengers who miss their flights. At airport gates, Agents announce flight departures and board passengers. They also ensure that flight attendants have the equipment they need.

Concessionaires / Airport Food Service Workers politely serve passengers at shops, newsstands, and food service companies located within the airport.

Airport Guides / Ambassadors provide assistance and information to airport passengers about the services available to them at the airport.

Airport Custodians / Servicepersons maintain lighting and perform janitorial work.

FINANCIAL MANAGEMENT

Christian Airport Managers, who may be Pastors, church or ministry leaders, or concerned, and committed individuals, typically operate as part of a church or other non-profit agency in accordance with the bylaws of the organization. Some, however, may be wealthy individuals, those with substantial influence, or perhaps even heads of families. To establish, stock, and operate their airports, a major aspect of their responsibilities consist of collecting donations from Stockholders. Funds donated are used for the purpose of fulfilling the airport's mission. In addition to monetary contributions, donations from shareholders also consist of supplies, which include, but are not limited to:

- Food

- Water for drinking, bathing, cooking, etc.

- Clothing, shoes

- Emergency generators, light bulbs, lenses and reflectors for runway markings, smoke detectors, fire extinguishers, smoke detectors, weapons, "Restricted Area" signs, surveillance equipment, warning signal system, whistles, battery operated televisions and radios, first aid and Emergency Response books, batteries, flashlights, over the counter medications, first aid supplies, masks, duct tape and other emergency supplies

- Bibles and other reading material

- Cots, bedding, towels

- Dishes, utensils, can openers, cookware, cooking and refrigeration apparatus

- Computers, copy machines, and office supplies, telephones and other electronic devices

- Grooming, hygiene, sanitary, laundry and cleaning supplies, garbage bags, storage containers, pest and rodent repellents

- Well maintained vehicles, aircraft, boats, trucks, and other modes of transportation, fuel, and tools for repairs

- Special items/provisions for infant, elderly, and disabled passengers

- Luxury items

- Etc.

AIRPORT EMERGENCY AND SAFETY OPERATIONS

Airports must assure passenger safety at all times; both in flight, and while at the airports. Regular inspections, restricted areas, security, maintenance, hazard, emergency, and disaster services are established to assure passenger safety. An airport emergency is any occasion or instance, natural or man-made, which warrants action to save lives and protect property and health. It is essential to prepare for emergencies that face an airport in order to be able to respond quickly and effectively. While every contingency cannot be anticipated and prepared for, a strong emergency preparedness program can assist in limiting the negative impact of these events. In the event of an emergency situation, the Airport's Emergency Plan is immediately activated. Emergency provisions include Emergency Medical Services, Aircraft Rescue and Fire Fighting, Hazardous Materials Response, National Weather/Natural Disaster Services, and Public Safety/Security.

TRANSPORTATION

Any vehicle authorized to operate on the airport runways, taxiways, or safety areas shall either be equipped with a radio, or shall be provided a hand held radio. Prior to entering these movement areas, the vehicle operator shall notify aircraft of his/her destination and purpose. Upon clearing the movement areas, he/she shall also notify Air Traffic Control to gain permission. Airports shall identify a designated location for vehicle parking, storage, and repairs. Airport facilities may not be equipped to provide other than minor or limited repairs, therefore, an adequate number of well-maintained vehicles must be available for use at all times. In order for flights to operate according to schedule, an adequate supply of fuel must be maintained at all times.

FLIGHT PLANNING

<u>Flight Plan Records</u>- Flight plan records, which generally include basic information such as departure and arrival points, estimated flying time, alternate airports to use in case of bad weather, type of flight, pilot's name, and number of people on board, are devised by the Airport Manager prior to the scheduling, ticketing, and booking of any flight. Each flight will have an assigned number. Flights are typically scheduled in accordance with passenger need, as it is the goal of each airport to ascertain that airplanes are filled to capacity. Each flight plan is provided to pilots prior to take-off to give them guidance and instructions for flying their aircraft, and to Air Traffic Control to enable them to initiate tracking and routing services and provide search and rescue operations, should it be required.

<u>Routing Types</u>- Aircraft routing types used in flight planning are:

- Airway routing, which occurs along pre-defined pathways

- Navaid, or Navigational Aids, which identify the point of airway intersection, allowing for changing from one airway to another

- Direct routes, where one or both of the endpoints is not located at a Navaid.

A route may be composed of segments of different routing type. For example, a route from Los Angeles to Rome may include Airway routing over the U.S. and Europe, but Direct routing over the Atlantic Ocean.

<u>Organized Tracks</u>- A series of paths similar to airways which cross ocean areas may be included in flight plans. Some tracks are fixed and appear on navigational charts and others change daily depending on weather and other unperceived dangerous factors, and therefore, cannot appear on printed charts.

AIRPORT OPERATIONS

<u>Booking Trips</u>- When we see Jerusalem being surrounded by armies, we know that desolation is near (Luke 21:20). At this time, we must ascertain that flight plans are developed, flights are assigned a flight number, passengers have booked their flights and obtained their itineraries and tickets, either through a ticket agent by phone, online via the airport's website, and/or, in the unfortunate event of inherent technological problems with phones, computers, and other electronic devices, in person, through assigned travel agencies at pre-determined times and locations.

<u>Flight Schedules</u>- Flight schedules are posted in airports to inform personnel and passengers of scheduled flights, and include the following information for each flight:

- Flight Number
- Routing (Departure and Arrival Locations)
- Departure Date and Time
- Arrival Date and Time
- Aircraft Type, including no aircraft (by foot)
- Number of Stops
- Delay Status, if Applicable

<u>Ticketing and Boarding Pass Procedures</u>- Although aviation services, like salvation, are free, passengers who walk in that Way (Isaiah 35:8) must receive their tickets, whether tangible or symbolic (a secret password, for example) in order to get on board and take flight. Extreme

measures are taken to ascertain that tickets obtained either online or offline through ticket counters and/or travel agencies, are issued only to qualifying passengers. For the safety of airport operations, airport security will ensure that only passengers will pass through the gates that were prepared for them by those who lovingly worked tirelessly to build up the highway; removing stones, and raising the banner (Isaiah 62:10 NIV).

In order to accomplish the mission of this Christian Airline, we must become and remain united, prayerful, watchful, and ready. Because these perilous end times leading up to the tribulation period will be exponentially more catastrophic and wicked than any other era in the history of mankind, our requirements for keeping watch and being ready for them will require specific, and much more intense secretiveness, planning, and preparation than any other event and time in history.

The harvest being ripe and plentiful, there is plenty of work for all servants of God, and no reason why, as long as God gives us grace and we are wise and faithful, we cannot unite to make our daddy proud by making arrangements to escape all that will happen, confidently receiving Him as our Savior when He arrives, while standing with our heads lifted high, and glorifying and marveling at Him. We must ask God to give us our specific end time task(s) and be sure to perform it/them with all diligence.

Those who wisely and faithfully watch for Him and give His great tribulation servants their food at the proper time, will be given a crown and great rewards by Jesus. Because we will have given others their food at the proper time, we will sit at God's table for His marriage supper and eat a feast of rich food that He, Himself will prepare and dress to serve us (Luke 12:37, Isaiah 25:6). If we rebuke the complacent and apathetic thinking regarding the end times and are faithful over these few things during a portion of our lives that are just fleeting vapors, we will share in His happiness for eternity, and be put in charge of many things. Therefore, let us love one another, unite as one people, keep watch, and be ready because truly, we ain't got long to stay here. God bless us all.

AS I AWAIT

As I await the glory of your presence,
As I await the smile upon your face,
As I await your gift of graceful eternity,
I'll stand firm with my head lifted high.

As I await to recline at your table,
As I await to be graciously served by you,
As I await for the room that you have prepared for me,
I'll stand firm with my head lifted high.

As I await to see the glory of your kingdom,
As I await to walk your streets of gold,
As I await to hear well done my faithful servant,
I'll stand firm with my head lifted high.

As I await for days of only sunshine,
As I await to see no death or pain,
As I await to take charge of your possessions,
I'll stand firm with my head lifted high.
I'll stand firm with my head lifted high.
I'll stand firm with my head lifted high.

REFERENCES

"Federal Aviation Administration." Federal Aviation Administration. N.p., n.d. Web. 12 Aug. 2015.

The Holy Bible, New International Version. Grand Rapids: Zondervan House, 1984. Print.

"The Underground Railroad." PBS. PBS, n.d. Web. 12 Aug. 2015.

Watkins, Terry. "Is the Biochip the Mark of the Beast?" Is the Biochip the Mark of the Beast? 666 WATCH, n.d. Web. 12 Aug. 2015.

MESSAGE FROM THE AUTHOR

P rayerfully, you have ears to have heard this profound, prophetic, and parabolic end time, physical assignment from God (Mark 13:34). If you did not hear the TOP SECRET, it is because God did not give you ears to hear it, so pray the prayer below, with your mouth and MEDITATE ON IT UNTIL YOU BELIEVE EVERY WORD OF IT IN YOUR HEART:

Heavenly Father: Thank you for sparing my life long enough for me to seek repentance for all of my sins. I realize that if I keep shunning your warnings and advice to turn from sin, the world, and the desires of my flesh, I am bound for hell. Please forgive me for all of my sins, and for closing my ears to you even though you have always been there for me; providing for me, protecting me, and forgiving me. I believe that you loved me enough to send your only begotten Son, Jesus Christ to this world to die for me, and that He was resurrected so that I can live forever in paradise with Him.

Help me on my Christian journey so that I do not fall away from you, but lead, guide, and teach me the way that I should go through your Holy Spirit. Help me to be more like You- loving, faithful, righteous, holy, obedient, peaceful, joyful, kind, caring, patient, gentle, self-controlled, and forgiving. Realizing that time is winding down fast, quickly mature me so that I can learn the lessons I need to learn in order to trust and obey You and be used by You more and more for the advancement of Your kingdom. Allow me to be a help on the road to my brothers and sisters, feeding them spiritually, physically, emotionally, mentally, financially, and in every other way possible. Thank you for receiving me into Your kingdom and for giving me ears to hear the message of Your TOP SECRET assignment, which I believe if you have not done so yet, that you will. I love You. I want to please You. And I offer up my life for Your sake on this day. Now use me for Your purpose. In Jesus' Name. Amen.

Jesus revealed the weightier matters to His disciples concerning the signs of the end times, which implicitly included His TOP SECRET assignment for us to prepare for our great tribulation flight to safety. He warned us to be watchful, ready, and prayerful that we would be able to escape all that is about to happen so that we will stand confidently before Him when He returns, as opposed to being sprawled out all over the earth, our carcasses being picked over by vultures.

Many continue to live in apathy, complacency, and fear, never giving the end times so much as a thought, let alone committing the subject to study and prayer. Due to the mass confusion, misinformation, ignorance, and arguments concerning the end times, even preachers commonly avoid the topic. This plainly written, and easily understood book, serves as an aid for churches, ministries, and those who truly believe that all biblical prophecy will continue to be exponentially revealed in frequency and intensity, like labor pains, until the end. Its timely purpose is to put an end to all arguing, fear-induced, panicky defeatism, doom, gloom, and dependence upon alleged timeframes associated with the last days and prepare servants of God for taking-off with our God ordained assignment before it is too late.

If God had an assignment for Noah and his family to build an Ark to survive the flood, and Moses, Harriet Tubman, and other abolitionists of the Underground Railroad to set the captives free and provide for their safety and protection, you can best believe He has a plan for us to build up an Ark of safety for His great tribulation saints to survive the horror of the end times.

www.ingramcontent.com/pod-product-compliance
Lightning Source LLC
LaVergne TN
LVHW051501070426
835507LV00022B/2870